TWISTED STRANDS

THE HIDDEN LEGACY OF WORLD WAR II, PART 2

CAROL SCHULTZ VENTO

SUNBURY
PRESS®

Mechanicsburg, PA USA

Published by Sunbury Press, Inc.
Mechanicsburg, PA USA

SUNBURY
P R E S S ®

www.sunburypress.com

For information about special discounts for bulk purchases, please contact Sunbury Press Orders Dept. at (855) 338-8359 or orders@sunburypress.com.

To request one of our authors for speaking engagements or book signings, please contact Sunbury Press Publicity Dept. at publicity@sunburypress.com.

FIRST SUNBURY PRESS EDITION: June 2024

Set in Adobe Garamond Pro | Interior design by Crystal Devine | Cover by Lawrence Knorr | Edited by Lawrence Knorr.

Publisher's Cataloging-in-Publication Data
Names: Vento, Carol Schultz, author.
Title: Twisted strands : the hidden legacy of World War II, part 2 / Carol Schultz Vento.
Description: Second trade paperback edition. | Mechanicsburg, PA : Sunbury Press, 2024.
Summary: *Twisted Strands* is a multidimensional narrative memoir which focuses on war, trauma, immigration, loss and redemption. It demonstrates the strength of the human spirit to overcome adversity.
Identifiers: ISBN : 979-8-88819-242-9 (paperback) | ISBN : 979-8-88819-243-6 (ePub).
Subjects: BIOGRAPHY & AUTOBIOGRAPHY / Military | HISTORY / Wars & Conflicts / World War II / European Theater | PSYCHOLOGY / Psychopathology / Post-Traumatic Stress Disorder (PTSD).

Designed in the USA
0 1 1 2 3 5 8 13 21 34 55

For the Love of Books!

To my Mother and Grandmothers,
who were role models of strong women.

To my Father,
who taught his daughter growing up in the fifties
that she could be anything she dreamed of being.

CONTENTS

Foreword *by Nancy Bowker*   vii

Foreword *by Christen Harty Schaefer*   ix

Author's Note   ix

Prologue   1

1.   Lucille—The Fulcrum   5

2.   Dudley the Unfortunate   10

3.   Fred the Savior   15

4.   Fort Bayard—The Meeting Place   19

5.   Mystery Man   22

6.   Dutch—Master of Reinvention   27

7.   Dutch & Mitzi—La Familia Meets the Wild West   43

8.   The Broken Family   49

9.   The Constancy of Change   55

10.   Forever Young (Bob Dylan)   61

11.   Conclusion   66

About the Author   70

FOREWORD

Behind those familiar and perhaps unknown names on our family trees are often shadows and mysteries. Sometimes, unsettling questions arise, such as, is this person the real parent? If this is true, will the revelation shatter who we thought we were? How did their choice to bury the truth affect who we are today?

This is the fascinating journey of *Twisted Strands*—Carol Vento's gripping deep dive exploration of her family's tangled roots. It's a compelling look into how long ago secrets impacted her sense of self and that of her valiant father, Arthur "Dutch" Schultz. His service as a paratrooper in World War II was noted in the landmark book, *Citizen Soldiers*, by Stephen Ambrose. He was also portrayed in the classic movie, *The Longest Day*.

I had the honor of speaking with Mr. Schultz on the telephone many years ago about an article he was working on. I had written articles and he wanted to run by me a few questions. He was so humble, yet his voice resonated with a strong force.

I could clearly feel how the character that had driven his heroic actions on D-Day and other battles had flowed into his daughter, Carol. Her strength of integrity throughout her own life's challenges has also infused her ability to tell a great story. Twisted Strands is a captivating portrait of the passion, betrayal, heartbreak and profound joy that are woven into the tapestry called family.

—Nancy Bowker, author of *John Raney: Horse Tamer, New Horse Handbook*, and *The Wild Horse: An Adopter's Manual*, co-authored by Barbara Eustis Cross

FOREWORD

This is the second time I've had the honor of being asked to write a foreword for Carol Schultz Vento. The first was for her book, *The Hidden Legacy of World War II: A Daughter's Journey of Discovery*, which focused on how the trauma of war impacted her family. That book and *Twisted Strands*, center on her wonderfully charismatic and complex father, Arthur Dutch Schultz, a World War II 82nd Airborne paratrooper who landed behind enemy lines in Normandy on D-Day. I met Dutch while directing a documentary on the making of Steven Spielberg's film *Saving Private Ryan*.

In *Twisted Strands*, author Carol Schultz Vento outdoes herself as she becomes a historical sleuth who courageously confronts the reality of generational trauma and blows open her family secrets. Through exhaustive research and sheer determination, she takes readers through a fascinating examination of her own family's complex narratives.

At just seventeen years old, Carol found herself in the unimaginable position of pleading with her sobbing father not to take his own life. "Thank goodness, I was supportive and just tried to talk him down," she shares with me. "Thank God, I told him he was a good dad, because I don't know what he would have done." At the time she had no idea where this despair came from. Five decades later she would set out to tackle her family's most harrowing heartaches to unravel the mystery of her father's origin.

As she lays out the clues chapter by chapter, she uncovers stories both heartbreaking and redemptive. From the lives of loved ones consumed by alcoholism, divorce and post-traumatic stress to the loss of her own two sisters, her intriguing memoir prompts the reader to consider the fractured legacies that may reside within their own family's past, inspiring a sense of responsibility to confront and heal those wounds.

Carol's journey points the way toward the possibility of transcendence—not just for her own family, but for all of us seeking to break the cycle of generational trauma. Carol's hard-won wisdom will undoubtedly inspire readers to embark on their own journeys of discovery, unearthing the hidden narratives that shape our identities and our futures. This book is a masterful testament to the power of personal reckoning, the resilience of the human spirit, and confronting our greatest fears. As Carol herself shares: *"Any bravery that I show is because of dad. He looked things straight in the eye and didn't sugarcoat reality. I figure that if he was brave enough to jump from an airplane when people were shooting at him, the least I could do was conquer my fear and put the story out there the way he would want."*

These days, when Carol babysits her precious granddaughter, she continues to tap into her ancestors' genes and channels her father's courage, reshaping intergenerational baggage and cultivating the beautiful hope of the future. I am profoundly grateful for her important work, as reading *Twisted Strands* has inspired me to do the same.

For those readers who believe that knowing your past is a clue to happiness in your future, this book is a roadmap of one woman's journey in that direction.

—Christen Harty Schaefer, writer and director of "Into the Breach: Saving Private Ryan" (HBO First Look)

AUTHOR'S NOTE

My father startled me with the unexpected news that the man I knew as Grandpop Schultz might not be my biological grandfather. A remark made to my father at Fred Schultz's San Diego, California funeral many decades ago won't let go of my psyche. The mystery of paternity, secrets, and intergenerational trauma fueled my quest for answers.

Dad, never quite sure of the truth concerning his paternity, posited that his biological father might have been his mother's first husband. He visited relatives in upstate New York; an elderly aunt told him, "We've been waiting for you." Armed with certainty, he hired a genealogist to create his family tree. Dad went to his resting place, assured that he had found his family.

In 2018, I wanted to find more relatives along this line, so I did an Ancestry DNA test. Using information obtained through genealogical research, DNA contacts, and sleuthing, I have been led down a winding and unexpected path consisting of two World Wars, a long-ago Spanish flu pandemic and the dreaded curse of tuberculosis, a disease long eradicated in the United States.

This book is a multigenerational narrative memoir based mainly on fact and placed in a historical context. Documentary evidence is available for all factual details, dates and important milestones. However, the emotional landscape and motivations of the people involved are based on my intuitive assumptions.

The impact of long-ago hidden decisions of my paternal grandparents played a significant role in my father's life and subsequently in my and my long-departed sister's life. Intergenerational trauma is part of the saga of three generations.

The names of my father, Arthur, and the nickname Dutch are used interchangeably throughout, as well as the names of my mother, Madeline, and the nickname Mitzi.

PROLOGUE

"War may sometimes be a necessary evil. But no matter how necessary, it is always an evil, never a good." —JIMMY CARTER[1]

War begets unlikely couplings and looms large in my life. In the aftermath of World War I, a deadly pandemic, and the dreaded disease of tuberculosis infecting his family, my father was born. In the immediate aftermath of World War II, in the first year of the baby boom, I entered the world. The amalgam of these global cataclysmic events not only influenced my father's existence but also mine. I have been on a search for genetic, emotional, and cultural clues about my heritage. As the only surviving child of three from my parents' broken wartime marriage, it is a solo and necessary journey for me to reconstruct the events of the past that have shaped me.

Finding my family roots is a path to understanding myself, as well as the forces that caused the early deaths of my sisters, one at two days and the other at 22 years.

Fueled by my curiosity and aloneness, it has become a passion to figure out where I fit. Family history and lore, genealogy, and DNA testing are my allies in this search. My maternal side is transparent; I'm the granddaughter of early twentieth-century Italian immigrants, and my genes and matching relatives confirm that. The mystery lies in my father's paternity.

It was at a long-ago funeral that questions arose . . .

Brotherly Love?

"The man in the casket is not your father." My uncle uttered those shocking words to my dad, Arthur 'Dutch' Schultz. In the mahogany

---

1. Nobel Peace Prize Lecture, December 10, 2002.

coffin laid my World War I Marine veteran grandfather, Frederick Ernest Schultz, dead at 69 in 1965.

The two brothers had competed relentlessly with each other since childhood. Arthur (aka Dutch),[2] age 42 in 1965, was a year older. He was handsome and charismatic with superb athletic skills. He overshadowed his younger brother, Ronald, especially in receiving attention from their mother, Lucille. In addition, Dutch's World War II service received widespread recognition with the publication of The Longest Day bestseller by Cornelius Ryan in 1959 and the subsequent 1962 blockbuster movie. Richard Beymer portrayed paratrooper Dutch Schultz's experiences when the scared young paratrooper jumped into Normandy on June 6, 1944.

Ronald was a World War II Marine who fought in the Pacific Theater at Guadalcanal, and there contracted malaria that debilitated him. No outsized attention was given to his valiant combat.

My uncle felt smug satisfaction at blindsiding his older brother. His allegation that Fred was not Arthur's biological father was based only on suspicion since Frederick Schultz was listed as the father on Arthur's 1923 birth certificate. Ronald's belief was based on access to Veterans' Administration records that he had while employed there. Lucille had been a World War I Army nurse, then subsequently a Public Health nurse at Fort Bayard, near Silver City, New Mexico. Her VA file (requesting VA benefits) revealed that she had, prior to marriage to Fred Schultz, married Douglas (Dudley) Sherman in a civil ceremony in Prescott, Arizona, on September 8, 1920. The couple's time together was short-lived. According to a divorce decree granted to Lucille on June 8, 1922, in Silver City, New Mexico, her divorce was based on desertion. She alleged Dudley had deserted her two months after their marriage. However, Lucille had waited more than eighteen months after the desertion to obtain a divorce, which complicated the paternity issue. She married Fred Schultz on December 7, 1922, five months after the final decree and only a month and a half prior to Arthur's birth at Saint Mary's Hospital in Phoenix, Arizona, on January 26, 1923. It's a fact that Lucille was still legally married to Sherman in late April or early May of 1922, at the probable time of Arthur's conception (based on his birth date).

---

2. My father was always called Arthur by his nuclear family; during his teen years he acquired the nickname Dutch, which is what everyone else called him.

Regardless of the absence of concrete proof, my uncle's words dumbfounded Arthur. Lucille was sitting mutely by her husband's casket, enveloped in grief. Her elder son crouched face to face with her, his piercing blue-green eyes awash in confusion. He asked his mother why she never mentioned that Fred might not be his biological father. She tersely responded, "You never asked," and refused to say more.

Questions with no answers—Did Lucille have an affair with Fred? Did she rendezvous with her husband, Dudley, one last time, even though the divorce papers stated they had been separated? At the time of Arthur's conception, Lucille had been a patient at Fort Bayard, New Mexico, for almost a year, an Army/Public Health hospital for tuberculosis patients, a disease that afflicted her after a month of nursing the TB patients there. She obtained the divorce in Silver City, close to Fort Bayard, while still a patient there. Could the biological father have been a patient or worker at the hospital?

The answers left with Lucille upon her demise in April 1966, a year after Fred's death. Would modern DNA testing provide the answer Lucille withheld? Dad often said that he "had to find himself," a search I had long believed was connected to his war trauma. Unbeknownst to him for much of his life, he didn't know the reason for his constant search for his identity. It wasn't only the impact of World War II; it was a secret about his paternity. It has been left to me to unravel the mystery of my father's origins and mine.

Understanding my father and the havoc his combat in World War II wrought upon our family was the impetus for my first book, *The Hidden Legacy of World War II: A Daughter's Journey of Discovery*. Through intensive research and plumbing the emotional depths of family trauma, many questions were answered.

But there remained the constant, nagging thought—why did my father react so strongly to war trauma, becoming an alcoholic for part of his life, with war memories bringing him to the brink of suicide? Why were other families of combat veterans relatively stable while ours was destroyed?

As I researched my World War I paternal grandparents' histories, it became clear the secrets and deceptions about dad's paternity were negative forces in his childhood, causing family dysfunction. Combined with his combat trauma from World War II, his children were impacted through two possible modes of transmission.

First, the scientific-based mechanism of epigenetics deals with the modification of genes. This modification happens as a result of occurrences in the person's environment. Chemical tags are "added or removed" from DNA, but there is no permanent change in the genome.[3]

There have been epigenetic effects discovered in children of parents who were traumatized through war, famine, the Holocaust, and child abuse.[4]

Second, the psychological theory of emotional inheritance focuses on a younger generation's carrying of past family trauma, even if their grandparents and parents never spoke of them. Galit Atlas, in her book *Emotional Inheritance*, notes, "The mind cannot prevent the psychological invasion of destructive aspects of the past."[5] Repression protects the person who experienced the trauma, but it is never fully processed and affects the next generation in the family.

According to Jeffrey Prager, "Traumatic expressions live beyond those who are direct recipients," causing "ghosts of the past to remain alive in children and grandchildren."[6] For example, children of Holocaust survivors often thought of themselves as protectors of their parents. As noted in this book, this process of parentification may also occur in the children of war veterans with PTSD.

Choices made by previous generations can cause unintended consequences for their children and grandchildren. This memoir illustrates that trauma does not end with those who are directly impacted.

3. "Can the Legacy of Trauma Be Passed Down the Generations?" BBC, 3/26/2019, BBC. com/future/article//20190326, accessed 10//18/22.

4. Stanley Krippner, Deidre Barrett, "Transgenerational Trauma: The Role of Epigenetics," *Journal of Mind and Behavior*, Winter 2019, Vol. 40, Number 1, pp. 53-62, www.jstor.org/ stable/26740747, accessed 10/10/22.

5. Galit Atlas, *Emotional Inheritance* (New York, Little, Brown Spark, 2022) 3.

6. Jeffrey Prager, "Danger and Deformation: Disrupting the Intergenerational Transmission of Trauma," *American Imago*, Vol. 72, No. 2 (Summer 2015), p.147, www.jstor.org/ stable/26305113, accessed 5/23/23.

1

LUCILLE—THE FULCRUM

"The greatest fine art of the future will be the making of a comfortable living from a small piece of land." —ABRAHAM LINCOLN[1]

My grandmother Lucille Barge Sherman Schultz was an imposing pioneer woman, 5'8" in stature, with a hazel-eyed penetrating stare, brownish gray thick braids atop her head, and a take-charge demeanor. When I was a child, I was both in awe and intimidated by her. She was born to homesteader parents in the Centennial state of Colorado on March 5, 1898, and grew up acclimated to the wilderness of the West. Her adventurous parents, Frank and Martha Ella Barge, had taken advantage of the federal Homesteading Act of 1862. As young marrieds, they made the life-altering decision to leave their small farm in Illinois in 1885. They were enticed by the opportunity to own 160 acres of undeveloped land in Fountain, Kit Carson County, Colorado. For their land ownership to be finalized within five years of arrival, a ten-foot by fourteen-foot residence must be built, and it had to be improved enough for the breadwinner to make a living from it. By November 6, 1890, Frank and Martha were successful in meeting the requirements and were "proved up" to obtain full ownership of the land. The Benjamin Harrison Presidential signed land patent certificate #7867 documenting ownership of section 3, 8S, 13W, Kit Carson County, was hung on their cabin wall.[2]

The Barges were successful at homesteading, unlike forty percent of those who had originally filed claims. Obstacles such as isolation, severe drought and other weather extremes did not deter them. The Barges had lost two young children, Clifton and Francis Arnold, prior to the birth

---

1. www.littleredacres.com/homesteading-quotes/.
2. Suzy Riding, "Pioneer History of Soapstone Prairie," 2019, City of Fort Collins, www.fc.gov, accessed 6/8/22.

of Lucille. By the time she was born on March 5, 1898, her parents had owned the homesteaded land for eight years. Lucille joined her ten-year-old sister Myrtle in the family, and two years after Lucille, in 1900, brother Jennings Bryan was born. It was a happy and rugged childhood on the open prairie. Lucille did her share of chores, cleaning the cabin and feeding the animals before and after her hours in a one-room school-house. Her older sister Myrtle was the designated driver to the school, traversing the five miles by horse and buggy. Lucille loved the kaleido-scopic and panoramic beauty of the prairie, collecting fossilized rocks and Native American Ute artifacts that beckoned her with their intricacy. During her early childhood, Frank Barge had procured a position with the Santa Fe Railroad as a construction foreman for a bridge and build-ing crew spanning a distance of 202 miles between La Junta, Colorado and Dodge City, Kansas. It was arduous, backbreaking work building and repairing dents, section houses, bridges and storage buildings. Frank lost his left arm in a gruesome accident in 1912 while constructing a pump house but stoically continued to work on the railroad until 1927.

Lucille's young world was tragically shattered with the death of her mother from cancer on November 22, 1910. Frank did not adjust to widowhood well and remarried again fairly quickly in December 1911. His new wife, Martha Elizabeth Cell King, was fourteen years younger than Frank and had been the subject of scandalous town gossip. She was a member of an established Fountain, Colorado family. Her father, David Cell, was a successful rancher, an early settler in the town in the mid-1870s.[3]

The gossip centered on her first marriage and its fateful ending. Mar-tha Elizabeth had previously been married to Silas King, a railroad switch operator. Their troubled, rancorous marriage lasted seven years and produced two children, Roland and Leona. Martha Elizabeth divorced Silas on November 25, 1907, after having him arrested for threatening to kill her. Shortly after their divorce, Silas accused Martha of marital infidelity, alleging she had an intimate relationship during her marriage with her employer, ranch owner William Johnson, for whom she was a housekeeper. Fueled by explosive rage and jealousy, he vowed revenge.

3. "Some History of Fountain from 1887," Historic Fountain Colorado, https://fountain-colorado.blogspot.com/search?q=David+cell, accessed 2/18/22.

On January 26, 1908, Silas arrived at the ranch and shot his former wife. Martha fell to the ground, stayed motionless, and faked being dead. A bullet had grazed her scalp and penetrated her shoulder. After seeing the blood from Martha's wounds, Silas believed he had murdered her. He then shot himself in the head. He bled profusely from a gaping would, lost consciousness and died three hours later.[4]

At the time of Martha Elizabeth's marriage to Frank in 1911, she had two young children, ages 9 and 5. She was not in the least bit interested in also parenting Frank's children, Lucille, age 13 and Jennings, age 11. Older sister Myrtle was married and out of the house. Frank callously sent his two younger children to a Catholic orphanage to be raised (likely Sacred Heart Orphanage in Pueblo, Colorado, run by Franciscan Sisters). According to family lore, Frank would take his two children from the orphanage in the summer to ride the Santa Fe rails with him while he was working but did not bring them to the home he shared with his wife and stepchildren. In 1913, Lucille, 15, and Jennings, 13, were living on their own in an apartment in Lamar, Colorado, where they attended school.

During her residence at Sacred Heart Orphanage, Lucille, raised Lutheran, converted to Catholicism due in part to the influence of the Franciscan Sisters. The nuns encouraged the intelligent, inquisitive girl to attend nursing school. In 1914, at 16, she began the nurse-training program at St. Mary's Hospital in Pueblo, Colorado. The timing was opportune for Lucille to become a nurse. In the early twentieth century, nurses were beginning to be trained in professional nursing programs instead of volunteering and apprenticing. The professional training field grew rapidly, and by 1917-18, there were 1,692 nursing schools associated with general hospitals.[5] On July 22, 1918, Lucille graduated from St. Mary's as a registered nurse.

During the time that Lucille was on her educational path to becoming a professional nurse, America entered World War I on April 6, 1917. Hostilities began in 1914 between the Allied Powers (Britain, France,

---

4. *Colorado Springs Gazette*, January 27, 1908, Newspaper Archive, https://newspaperarchive.com/colorado-springs-gazette-jan-27-1908-p-11.

5. H.R. Bonner, "Nurse Training Schools," 1917-18, Bulletin, 1919, No. 73, Bureau of Education, Department of the Interior, https://eric.ed.gov/?id=ED541382, accessed 4/15/22.

Russia, and Serbia) and the Central Powers (Germany, Austria, Otto-
man Empire). Victory for the Allies was elusive. They were battered and
decimated until the United States joined the fight on April 2, 1917.
There was finally a large infusion of fresh troops to aid the exhausted and
depleted Allied Forces.

Shortly after Lucille's graduation, she joined the Red Cross to help in
the war effort, as documented by her Red Cross Nursing Service Card.
Wanting to do more to help wounded and sick soldiers, she entered the
Army Nurse Corps on October 1, 1918, when she was twenty.

Lucille began her stint as an Army nurse at the intersection of two
global crises: war and the Spanish flu pandemic. World War I ended on
November 11, 1918, shortly after her entrance into the Army. The combat death toll for the American military in "the war to end all wars" was
53,402. However, death from Spanish Influenza ravaged the American
troops, with mortality from that plague estimated at 55,000, exceeding
fatalities from battle.[6]

Army nurses were on the front lines of treatment for wounded men,
but also for those afflicted with the highly contagious Spanish flu. The
disease quickly progressed from fever, sore throat, and headache to hem-
orrhagic pneumonia. It was a pre-antibiotic world, so care provided by
the nurses consisting of ice packs, nutritious food, and hydration were the
only remedies. Even though patients in military hospitals were isolated,
the disease spread quickly. A soldier could be in robust health, decline
suddenly and die rapidly. The most at-risk group in this pandemic were
young adults aged twenty to forty, the age group of the majority of the
military male patients and female nurses.

For her initial Army nursing assignment, Lucille was sent to Fort
Douglas, Utah, at the beginning of October 1918. Only a month later,
in November, she fell ill with Spanish flu, the overarching occupational
hazard for many Army nurses. She was a patient at the base hospital for
a week, then isolated in nurses' quarters for two weeks. Prior to being
infected with Spanish flu, she had been in robust health, as affidavits

6. Carol R. Byerly, Ph.D., *The U.S. Military and the Influenza Pandemic of 1918-19*, Public
Health Rep., 2010, 125 (Supp 13): 82-91, www.ncbi.nlm.nih.gov/pmc/articles,PMC2862337.
* Note: Information on Lucille Barge Sherman Schultz was accessed from her Veterans
Administration file which Dutch Schultz received a copy of in 1995.

from her VA files demonstrate. However, she suffered severe lingering effects from her illness, including pleurisy, fatigue and lack of stamina.

Unable to perform her nursing duties, she was honorably discharged from the service on July 18, 1919. After a short period of rest at home in Colorado, she wanted to return to nursing and applied for readmission to the Army Nurse Corps on September 19, 1919, but was denied due to being over the age limit (she was 21 at that time). Determined to return to nursing, she applied and received an appointment with the United States Public Health Service on August 1, 1920. She first worked at St. Vincent's Hospital in Santa Fe, New Mexico. After a short break to rest up, she began work at Fort Whipple in Prescott, Arizona, previously an Army hospital, which had been designated a Public Health Service hospital for World War I veterans with tuberculosis.

Her tenure at Fort Whipple was short. It was a place that loomed large in her life, however, because she became romantically involved with a patient hospitalized there, a New Englander, Douglas (Dudley) Sherman.

2

DUDLEY THE UNFORTUNATE

"Men are not prisoners of fate, but of their own minds." —FDR[1]

Douglas (aka Dudley) Sherman was an unlucky man. On February 22 in the year 1898, he was born in Whitingham, Vermont, a picturesque rural community nestled in the Green Mountains. His parents were a mismatched couple. His father, Allison Drury Sherman, was a forty-six-year-old merchant and postmaster. His mother, Ruth May Flora, was a seventeen-year-old girl at the time of the marriage ceremony, officiated by the groom's father, Nathan Drury Sherman. Nathan was a proper Unitarian Universalist minister who had performed hundreds of weddings and funerals in the town and surrounding communities. On her September 1, 1897, wedding day, Ruth was five months visibly pregnant. The union assured them that Douglas would not be illegitimate. It is unknown whether Allison was the biological father of the child. It's possible that the teenage Ruth was a servant in one of the Sherman households. The scandal of an out-of-wedlock pregnancy in a prominent minister's family was unacceptable in late nineteenth-century New England.

Their implausible marriage was short-lived. By 1900, according to census records, Allison was divorced from his wife. Ruth was living close to the Vermont border, in the Massachusetts household of her father, Dudley Flora, according to the census data. The census also documented the existence of a four-month-old baby, Charles, as Dudley Flora's grandson, with Ruth likely the mother. There is no evidence of Douglas (aka Dudley) being there; the census records suggest he may have been living with his uncle, Elijah Flora and his family. Sadly, before the toddler had a chance to bond with his mother, he lost her completely. Ruth

---

1. "Hands off the Western Hemisphere" speech, 1939, The Public Papers and Addresses of Franklin Delano Roosevelt, 1939 vol., *War and Neutrality.*

died at nineteen during the epidemic of typhoid fever in North Adams, Massachusetts.

Dudley lived with maternal family members during his childhood years and didn't appear to have a relationship with his purported father. He spent most of those years with his mother's brother, Elijah, who labored on one of the local farms. Dudley was a slight boy at 17, 5'6", with a lean, wiry frame. As a teenager, he worked at basket weaving, an unusual occupation for a non-Native American at the time. Typically, the basket weavers in New England and the Northeast were often itinerant peddlers, selling to farmers. It was a hard life with meager monetary rewards.[2]

World affairs intrigued Dudley. World War I began on July 28, 1914. England entered the war on August 4th of that year, and Canada was automatically involved in the fighting; America held back from joining the hostilities. Dudley must have considered being in the military during wartime a better endeavor than itinerant basket weaving. He volunteered for the Canadian Army and enlisted in Toronto on June 7, 1916. He was assigned to the 1st Construction Battalion having high hopes for overseas action.

However, continuing Dudley's path of unlucky circumstances, he never did cross the ocean. Soon after enlisting, he was stricken with tuberculosis. He had tested positive and suffered the associated symptoms of malaise, weakness, coughing, and spitting up blood. By August 8, 1916, the Canadian Army's recommendation was to transfer him to a TB sanitarium. By October 1916, he was at the Mountain Sanitarium in Hamilton, Ontario, Canada. He was isolated from the community at large, and his two-month military career and dreams of an escape were put on hold. TB was a feared disease in the early twentieth century, and those afflicted were shunned. The sanitariums were well maintained, and patients received excellent care, even with the isolation from the "healthy." The farmland on many sanitarium sites enabled staff and patients to grow their own food, weather permitting.

After a year and a half at Mountain Sanitarium, Dudley was transferred to Spadina Military Hospital in Toronto, Ontario, Canada. According to his medical records, tests showed no active tuberculosis at that

2. Canyon Wolf, "19th Century Basket Making in New England," *The Ne-DO-Ba Research Journal*, September 7, 2011, https://wolf-trails.blog, accessed 5/20/22.

time. However, he was diagnosed as suffering from "debility," defined in that era as weakness or feebleness. Debility was often associated with a quiescent tuberculosis nilus infection, which could cause symptoms. Dudley also had the dreaded venereal disease of gonorrhea, which was resolved with treatment at the hospital.

Plagued with illness, Dudley never left North America during his time in the Canadian military. Since the bulk of his service had been spent in medical facilities, it was determined that he be medically discharged. This occurred on November 9, 1918, two days prior to the end of World War I.

Physical woes continued after his release from the Canadian Army. He made his way to the western United States. Upon his arrival in Phoenix, Arizona, he was promptly admitted to St. Luke's Home in the desert. The facility was a "thoroughly equipped sanitarium" for the treatment of TB run by the Episcopal Church. The price was set according to the need and financial ability of the patient.[3] The medical staff at St. Luke's diagnosed him with moderately advanced TB in both lungs. Dudley remained at St. Luke's from December 1918 until September 1919, when he was discharged.

He wandered around the desert for six months until TB struck again. Early 1920 found him further west in northern California in a U.S. Public Health Service Hospital at Menlo Park, San Mateo County. The federal government created public Health Service hospitals. The expansion of these hospitals was prolific in the 1920s. The goal was to serve the needs of the poor and needy, including those who had been afflicted by TB and other contagious diseases of the era, such as smallpox.

After a short stay in California, Dudley was transferred back to a hospital in Arizona at Fort Whipple in Prescott, Arizona. The former Army barracks/World War I hospital was on loan to the U.S. Public Health Service from 1920 to 1922. This site had previously been an Army hospital for military and veterans with TB that had focused on the same mission as its successor public health service hospital.

Dudley's hospitalization at Whipple from March 1920 to September 1921 coincided with my grandmother Lucille's arrival there as a Public

3. "Finding Aid to St. Luke's Home. Sanatorium, Hospital, and Health System," *MG 39*, Historical Note, www.arizonahistoricalsociety.org, accessed 5/12/23.

Health Service nurse. She had begun this nursing employment in August 1920 after she was denied readmission to the Army Nurse Corp due to being overage at 21. There must have been a strong, immediate, mutual attraction between Dudley and Lucile since they married in Arizona on September 8, 1920, barely a month after Lucille's arrival. The marriage was in haste; the reason is unknown. Dudley and Lucille left Fort Whipple and Prescott and moved to Los Angeles, California. By October of 1920, Dudley had abandoned Lucille. She was alone in Los Angeles and frantically figuring out her next move. Meanwhile, Dudley next appeared at the Barlow Sanitarium in early 1921, a TB hospital in Chavez Ravine in the Los Angeles environs.

Lucille, after her husband's desertion, moved on with her life. She soon left Southern California and traveled north 500 miles to French Creek, obtaining nursing employment at San Joaquin General Hospital.

Perhaps the marriage to Lucille was the high point of Dudley's life. He lived a transient existence for many years after 1921-22, never to marry again. From 1922 to World War II, he held various low-paying jobs, including dishwasher, supply man, elevator operator and junior clerk. His living situation ranged from homelessness to cheap rooming houses. In an application to the Veteran's Administration to obtain disability payments, Dudley's own words described his existence, noting that he had left the medical world behind in 1922. "Western sunshine, mountain and desert air, with what good food I've been able to obtain in my limited physical capacity, have been the only medical agencies I've been able to consult, often finding myself in a hobo's realm for months at a period." (Pension questionnaire-Los Angeles VA Regional Office-1947). The WWI Canadian Army veteran was able to petition the US Veterans Administration because he had served stateside in America for eight months during WWII. He had volunteered for the U.S. Army shortly after Pearl Harbor in early 1942 when he was 44 and was honorably discharged as a private in March 1943 at Camp Beale, California. After his stay in the Army with "3 hots and a cot," he returned to the dire circumstances he had left behind.

The VA disability request was denied because no active TB was found in 1947, even though Dudley claimed symptoms of fever, weight loss, cough and night sweats. He borrowed money from friends to live in the ensuing years while also working low-income jobs and occasionally receiving state disability insurance payments.

Lucille wanted to find Dudley's whereabouts more than three decades after their marriage. She hired the Tracers Company of America in 1952 to investigate the location of Dudley. The report noted that "he had been moving from one poor type rooming house to another," residences that were described in the letter to Lucille as "flea-bag."[4] Lucille and Dudley had been divorced since June 8, 1922, in Silver City, New Mexico, on the grounds that Dudley had "wholly deserted and abandoned" Lucille.[5] It is unknown whether Lucille and Dudley had contact with each other from 1922 on and, if so, what had transpired during any possible meeting of the two.

Dudley's life came to a lonely, sad end on April 26, 1961. He died at a Los Angeles Veterans Administration Hospital after being admitted on March 14, 1961, with a diagnosis of cancer of the left lung. His death was noted on his death certificate as "carcinoma of the abdomen with metastases to lungs, bilateral." Notification was made to his landlady, Alfreda Clark, who was listed as his contact person. The information she provided was that Dudley had no known living relatives; his younger brother Charles had died in 1949. He was buried on May 2, 1961, in the VA cemetery, with a few friends attending the service. The interment flag normally presented to relatives of the deceased was returned to stock. The unlucky life of Dudley Sherman was finally over.

4. Letter to Lucille Schultz, June 13, 1952, Tracers Company of America, 515 Madison Avenue, New York, New York.

5. Divorce Decree, *Lucille Sherman, Plaintiff vs. Douglas Sherman, Defendant*, in the District Court of the Sixth Judicial District of the State of New Mexico, within and for the County of Grant. *Note: Information about Douglas "Dudley" Sherman was accessed from a genealogy report Dutch Schultz received in 1994 and also from records accessed on Ancestry.com.

3

FRED THE SAVIOR

"Gas! Gas! Quick, boys! An ecstasy of fumbling
Fitting the clumsy helmets just in time,
But someone still was yelling and stumbling
And flound'ring like a man in fire or lime."
—WILFRED OWEN[1]

Grandpop Fred was a kind, gentle soul whose demeanor belied the hardships he had endured. The backstory of his complicated paternity, shellshock, and heroism in World War I was unknown to me for many decades.

Frederick Ernest Reddig was born in Berlin, Germany, on April 10, 1895, to 25-year-old Marie Reddig, a maid in the well-to-do Leist household in the capital city of the German Empire. Marie had left her home in Bischofsburg, East Prussia (now Biskupier, Poland) after her cobbler father died prematurely. She traveled 418 difficult miles to find employment in the big city.

While working as a domestic for the family, Marie was "taken advantage of" (family history) by a Leist son and became pregnant. After Fred's out-of-wedlock birth, the Leist family wanted custody of the child. Fearing her son would be taken from her, Marie fled first to her Prussian family home and soon thereafter left Germany in 1896 with her baby for America. She found a safe haven at the San Francisco home of her older sister, Elizabeth, who had come to the United States in 1894 to wed Valentine Ehrmann in an arranged marriage.

Shortly after Marie and Fred joined the Ehrmann household, a handsome visitor appeared. The guest was Valentine's friend Alfonso (Al) Zanon.

---

1. "Dulce et Decorum Est" in *Poems* (Viking Press, 1921).

Al was an immigrant like Marie and the Ehrmanns. He was born in 1859 in the town of Camp Denn, Tyrol, the bucolic region on the border of Italy and Austria. At the time of his birth, the area was part of Austria (Austria later ceded the Tyrol region to Italy in 1919 after World War I). Al had been influenced during his boyhood by the diverse cultures of both countries. He was fluent in German and Italian and became proficient in English after he emigrated to America with his two brothers in 1878. Successful at prospecting, he rejoiced in a major strike of silver and lead at Cooke's Peak, part of the Mimbres Mountain Range, 17 miles from the town of Deming, New Mexico. (His strike was valued at approximately $80,000 (Deming, New Mexico Headlight, May 2, 1974). After the strike, Al settled in Deming with his brothers. The three Zanon brothers took over the Schultz silver and lead mine after the three unlucky Schultz brothers were killed in an Indian raid (according to family lore). Thereafter, the Zanon brothers were called the Schultz brothers and took that name as their own. Prior to 1906, there was no law requiring name changes to be documented during naturalization proceedings. The Schultz name has persisted through the family line for four generations at this time.

Life in Deming, New Mexico, at the turn of the century, was a mixture of tradition and progress. During the Industrial Revolution, Deming became a minor railroad hub, being an intersection of Southern Pacific and Atchinson, Topeka, and Santa Fe Railroads; however, the Native American (Mimbres tribe) and Wild West influences were still prominent.

Al was a thirty-seven-year-old bachelor, and he fell in love with Marie while visiting the Ehrmann household. Within three weeks of their initial meeting, he married her. Al, Marie, and young Fred then left San Francisco to travel to Deming. Marie, upon arriving in the town, stated, "What a godforsaken place this is!" as she surveyed the inhabitants and the mountain vista. (Family history, Elizabeth Schultz Reese)

Fred grew up in Deming, taking the Schultz surname since Al was raising him as his son. Fred, being so young, was not aware that Zanon/Schultz was not his biological father. Not until 1942, at the start of WWII when the FBI was investigating him for a classified position, did he know that he wasn't born in Deming and Al was his stepfather. Even though Deming, N.M. census records of 1900 and 1910 state Fred was a stepson born in Germany, Fred in his WWI draft registration and 1930 and 1940 census stated he was natural-born in Deming, New Mexico). He had to legally change his name from Leist to Schultz in a court proceeding at that time.)

The Schultz family expanded with the birth of Fred's half-brother, Carl, in 1910. Fred was a teenager, and he began traveling the country on his own. He was living in Detroit in 1917 when he presented his application to join the Marine Corps. The WWI standards for recruiting required applicants to be citizens, unmarried, with no dependents, and in good health as to senses and limbs. Fred met all the categories except citizenship, but as noted above, that fact was discovered at a much later date. At enlistment, he was considered a prime candidate and officially became a Marine when he arrived at Parris Island, South Carolina, on January 2, 1918.

Boot camp was rigorous. Training consisted of eight weeks of intensive training, including bayonet fighting, close order drills, physical combat, and wall climbing. The final three weeks were devoted to marksmanship. Fred qualified as a marksman in March 1918.[2]

Fred's journey to war in Europe began with a departure from the Philadelphia Naval Yard on April 25, 1918. He arrived in mid-May in Brest, France. The fiercest battle of WWI was on the horizon—Belleau Wood, an area close to the Marne River in France. This bloody, iconic battle, which lasted almost a month from June 1 to June 26, helped turn the tide of the war against the Germans during their 1918 spring offensive. The victory, however, was costly for the Americans, with many Marines and soldiers killed. Fred was in the 5th Marine Regiment that had earned the nickname "Devil Dogs" for relentlessly battling the Germans while being severely outnumbered and successfully halting a German advance towards Paris. The Marines were poorly supported by attached French troops. The casualties were enormous: 2000 dead and 8000 injured Marines. Bayonet fighting, fierce hand-to-hand combat, shrapnel, and gunshots were responsible for many of the casualties.[3]

2. "Preparing for War," MCRD Parris Island, www.mcrdpi.marines.mil/Portals/76/Docs/centennialcelebrationbook, accessed 1/14/23.

3. "U.S. Marines and Allies Mark 104th Anniversary of Belleau Wood, 29 May 2022," The Official United States Marine Corps Public Website, www.marines.mil/News-Display/Article/3046879.

My grandfather was shot in the forehead during combat on June 10th, 1918. He rejoined his unit in Belleau Wood after a short recovery from the gunshot wound. Unfortunately, he was doused with mustard gas on July 19, 1918. Mustard gas was toxic to the body. As a killing agent, it would blister "the lungs and throat if inhaled in large quantities," causing a gruesome death if a gas mask was not worn. Masked Marines and soldiers also suffered from their skin horribly burning and blistering when the gas soaked and contaminated their woolen uniforms.[4]

The extent of injuries due to the gassing of Fred was not documented in his military records. However, he was immediately evacuated to the hospital.

The proportion of mustard gas fatalities to total casualties was low— only two percent of mustard gas victims died. However, the poison gas caused lifelong scars, both on the skin and in the lungs. Affected lung tissue was very susceptible to tuberculosis.[5]

Fred rejoined his Marine unit 6 weeks after his gassing. His health declined due to the aftereffects of mustard gas, and he received an honorable medical discharge due to "poison gas" on April 30, 1919, upon the recommendation of the Board of Medical Survey. The toxic exposure and lung scarring contributed to his eventually contracting tuberculosis. He returned to Deming an ill man. His stay at home was short; soon, he was sent fifty miles north from his family to a tuberculosis sanitarium in the New Mexico desert. It was here at Fort Bayard that the worlds of Fred and Lucille collided.

---

4. Marek Pruszewicz, "How Deadly was the Poison Gas of WWI?," BBC News, 30 Jan. 2015, www.bbc.com/news/magazine-3102472#

5. Harry L. Gilchrist, M.D., and Philip B. Matz, M.D., "Veterans at Risk: The Health Effects of Mustard Gas and Lewisite," Excerpt from *The Residual Effects of Warfare Gases* (1933), www.ncbi.nlm.nih.gov/books/NBK236056/.

4

FORT BAYARD—THE MEETING PLACE

"Veterans returning from the First World War with tuberculosis were often shunned and sent off to isolated sanitarium."
—Tom MacGregor[1]

Dutch's beginnings were in a former military outpost transformed into a tuberculosis sanitarium. Situated in an isolated area of New Mexico. Fort Bayard was originally established on August 21, 1866, in the aftermath of the Civil War. The post in Southwestern New Mexico had been commissioned at the height of the Indian with the goal of taking possession of Apache land for expansion of the United States westward. Buffalo Soldiers (125th U.S. Colored Troops, Company F) were ordered to protect mining camps and frontier settlers from attacks by Indians. The Native Americans were resisting the government's seizure of their land and homes and their forced settlement in reservations. The outpost was named for a Civil War general, George Bayard, who was killed at the Battle of Fredericksburg in 1862.

By 1899, there was no need for a military fort. The Indian wars had ended with the Apache moving into distant reservations and the vanquishing of the land rights of Native Americans. Bayard was converted into an Army tuberculosis hospital. The location, with mountain air, low humidity and abundant sunshine, was considered beneficial to healing for tuberculosis patients. This disease accounted for approximately twenty percent of American deaths in 1900 and was a leading cause of death in America. (www.circulatiynow.nim.nih.gov) Extremely ill patients were brought to the sanitarium by mule-drawn ambulances upon their arrival at the nearby Southern Pacific train station in Silver City.

---

1. "The lonely fight of the tuberculosis veterans," *Legion Magazine*, October 8, 2017.

During the tenure and direction of Colonel George Bushnell, Army Medical Corps, the facility experienced tremendous growth. There were 70 wood and brick buildings, including stately doctors' houses, nurses' quarters, maintenance facilities and two hospital buildings. Bushnell's credo was that beauty aided in healing. The grounds had a variety of colorful foliage and flowers many trees like pine and cedar, which were native to the area. An outdoor oasis of beauty surrounded the patients as they basked in the sunlight.[2]

In 1919, Fort Bayard was transferred from the Army to the United States Public Health Service. In 1922, it came under the control of the newly formed Veterans Bureau. Lucille entered Fort Bayard in August 1921 as a Public Health nurse during this transition period. She had recovered well from her bout with Spanish Influenza and subsequent TB to return to nursing duties, although not as an Army nurse after her medical discharge because she was deemed overage at 21. She was mainly on the night shift with the responsibility to care for severely ill patients. However, by November 1921, she experienced significant weight loss and had a persistent cough. The examination by the hospital Medical Officer revealed tuberculosis.

She was immediately released from her nursing job and placed in the infirmary for complete bed rest.

She remained at Fort Bayard for almost a year, mostly as a patient. During her medical stay, she met the man who would eventually become her second husband, Fred Schultz. Fred had been a TB patient there, and he and Lucille became friendly. He was transferred to Letterman Army General Hospital in San Francisco, where he also was treated for shell shock caused by his combat experience in World War I. Lucille and Fred kept in regular touch by letter after he departed from Bayard. During Lucille's stay at the sanitarium, she decided to rid herself legally of her first husband, Dudley Sherman. She petitioned the court in nearby Silver City, New Mexico, for a divorce on the grounds of desertion by Dudley. The complaint alleged they had not lived together since late 1920. The decree was granted on June 8, 1922.

On June 30th, 22 days after the finalization of her divorce, she left Fort Bayard against the medical advice of her doctors. However, the

---

2. David Pike, "Faded Glory," *New Mexico Magazine*, Sept. 1, 2016, www.newmexicomaga-zine.org/blog/post/fort-bayard.

doctors did not resist since Lucille was a nurse and could follow medical advice on her own. At the time of her departure, she still suffered from active tuberculosis and likely realized that she was pregnant (based on the birth date of my father, the date of his conception occurred in early May 1922). There is no indication in Lucille's medical records that the physicians were aware of her pregnancy. The assumption is that Lucille wanted to keep that information secret out of shame and confusion. My father, Arthur Dutch Schultz, was the result of that pregnancy, being born full term on January 26, 1923, in Phoenix, Arizona.

Arthur's beginnings are shrouded in mystery. Lucille was still legally married to Dudley Sherman in early May. Even though the grounds for divorce were desertion, is it possible that the two could have rendez-voused before the divorce was finalized?

Could Fred have visited Fort Bayard in early May? There is no indication in his military records of his dates of hospitalization and discharge from Letterman. Fort Bayard patient records are not available for dates after 1919. However, my father obtained Lucille's VA records many years ago. Detailed information on her time at Fort Bayard was included in the material.

My father went to his grave believing that Dudley Sherman may have been his biological father after discovering that Fred was not.

Lucille and Fred somehow reunited after she left Fort Bayard in late June. They married on December 7, 1922, when Lucille was seven and a half months pregnant. Fred and Lucille had moved to Phoenix, Arizona, for the climate before the birth since they both still had active tuberculosis. Arthur was born at Saint Mary's Hospital on January 26, 1923. Fred's name is listed as Arthur's father on the birth certificate as he was Lucille's husband at that point.

The question of Dudley or Fred took an unexpected turn when I sent my DNA to Ancestry. It made my search very confusing since my matches were to neither of the men. I matched my grandmother Lucille's relatives, but the biological grandfather's line was a mystery since I had a multitude of matches with ancestors whose names I did not recognize. According to Ancestry DNA analysis, my ancestors on that line were from the Deep South states of Alabama, Mississippi, Louisiana and East Texas. An exploration of the heritage of ancestors of whom I had no knowledge or awareness ensued.

5

MYSTERY MAN

"What happens when who you thought your parent was turns out to be a lie . . . Confusion, pain and undue shame . . . all effects of trauma." —MEREDITH GORDON RESNICK[3]

Understanding my father and the havoc his combat in World War II wrought upon our family was the impetus for *The Hidden Legacy of World War II: A Daughter's Journey of Discovery.* Through intensive research and plumbing the emotional depths of my family's traumas, many questions were answered.

However, there was the constant, nagging thought—why was my father so shattered by war that he became an alcoholic and teetered on the brink of suicide? Many other combat veteran fathers who I knew were stable and able to put the war behind them. Their families weren't destroyed by war like ours was.

As I was doing paternal family genealogical research to discover more about my grandparents and their forbearers, it became clear that there were secrets and deceptions in the Schultz saga.

My paternal grandparents, both World War I veterans, were complicit in hiding the truth about my father's paternity. Even after the bombshell revelation at Fred Schultz's funeral that he was not Dutch's biological father, my grandmother would not divulge information, responding only to dad's question as to why she didn't tell him by tersely saying, "You never asked."

My father then embarked on his search for answers with limited information. He assumed that Lucille's first husband, Dudley Sherman, was his birth father since Lucille was still legally married to him at the

---

3. "When Who You Thought Your Parent Was Turns Out to Be a Lie," *Psychology Today,* November 16, 2020.

time of conception. Dad and his siblings all went to their graves, believing Sherman was the father. My genealogist aunt included the Sherman line in her trees.

I looked for Sherman DNA matches but found only one sixth-cousin match. But oddly, I had a multitude of matches with ancestors whose names I didn't recognize. Those ancestors were from the South, mainly in the states of Louisiana, Alabama, Mississippi and Texas, not from New England or New York, where the Sherman and Flora families had settled. It was clear that Dudley Sherman was not my biological grandfather. My father had falsely assumed that since my grandmother was legally married to Sherman at the time of conception, Dudley had to be his father, even though the Sherman-Barge divorce document a few months after Lucille became pregnant stated the Dudley had deserted her more than a year earlier. When my father went to meet Sherman relatives in New York in the late 1960s, they greeted him warmly as a lost family member. However, they had no contact with Dudley for decades after his brother Charles died in 1949. To the remaining relatives, it was conceivable that Dudley had a child of whom no one was aware. I even connected with a second cousin on the Sherman line who shared genealogical information with me.

I once again had to come to terms with the fact that I had no idea who my biological grandfather was. First, I lost the biological connection with Fred, who I considered my true grandfather by love if not blood. Then, all the information that my dad had given me and the contacts I had along the Sherman line were irrelevant, leading me to question not only parts of my identity but also the impact the continuing lies had on my father.

In 2020, I contacted a third cousin DNA match, asking if she knew how I was related to her. Her answer broke my genealogical logjam. I was her relative on her Cooper line, a family that had been early settlers in St. Tammany Parish in Louisiana, having moved there from North Carolina.

Another third cousin's DNA match helped me fill in an additional branch of my family tree, linking me to the Taylor line, which originated in the Carolinas during colonial times and settled mainly in Texas.

Going back five generations on Ancestry Thru lines, I had 145 matches on the Cooper line and 54 on the Taylor line. The high number of matches with consistent trees confirmed that there was a strong family connection, but I still had no idea who my paternal biological grandfather was. I began working from my closest DNA matches, who were second cousins and was able to determine the probable identity of my great grandparents, the paternal line being Taylor and the maternal line Cooper.

Since my father had been a paratrooper in World War II and stayed in the Army as a counterintelligence agent for many years, I began to look at the Cooper and Taylor ancestors for military service. Serendipitously, I found an ancestor, my 6th great-grandfather, William Austin Cooper, who had been a scout for Daniel Boone. My father had been a scout for the 82nd Airborne in his war. William Austin had also been instrumental in building Fort Nashborough, which was the site of the future city of Nashville, Tennessee. He and his Chickasaw Native American wife, Malea, died in 1781, defending the fort from the attack of the Chickamauga Cherokee led by Chief Dragging Canoe.[4] A number of Cherokee tribes joined with the British during Revolutionary time to stop white settlers from encroaching on their territory.[5]

William Austin and Malea's son, my 5th great grandfather, Cornelius I Cooper, who lived in Georgia, was a soldier in Ore's regiment, a post-Revolutionary War militia in Territory South of the Ohio.

Fourth great-grandfather Cornelius M. Cooper was an early pioneer along the Bogue Chitto River. One of the first settlers in 1812 in the small town of Sun at the top of St. Tammany Parish, Louisiana, he fought valiantly as a private in the Battle of New Orleans and lived a long life practicing medicine after the war. Many of his descendants remained in the area and hundreds of them gathered together in 1955 to commemorate the placing of a monument atop his grave in the Old Cooper Cemetery.[6]

The Cooper line merged with the Taylor line with the marriage of my great-grandparents. Fanny Cooper and Thomas Monroe Taylor, a union

4. "Fort Nashborough," Memories Matter, April 13, 2022, https://memories-matter.blog/2022/04/13/.

5. "A Cherokee war campaign against the southern colonies begins," The Revolutionary War and Beyond, www.revolutionary-war-and-beyond.com, accessed10/15/23.

6. "The History of Sun," Tammany Family, August 2, 2018, https://tammanyfamily-blogspot.com/search?q=Cornelius+Cooper
    accessed 7/28/23.

that most likely produced my paternal grandfather, according to a number of DNA matches I have. There are second cousins I am related to who have the same great-grandparents as I do. Fanny Cooper has a notable ancestor who served in the Revolutionary War. Captain Francis Stringer fought in The Battle of Yamacraw Bluff, also known as The Battle of the Rice Boats. The Savannah River, between the Province of Georgia and the Province of South Carolina, was the locale for the land and naval battle between the Patriots/colonists and the British Royal Navy over food provisions. The colonial rebels were partly successful in ensuring the British did not achieve their goal of obtaining all the provisions. Francis Stringer survived that battle but died two years later, possibly in battle, but there is no documentation of that.

The paternal Taylor line also had at least one Revolutionary War ancestor. My 5th great grandfather, Captain Leroy Taylor, was a member of the North Carolina regiments from 1776 to 1779, and some of his direct descendants fought in the War of 1812.

The paternal genetic heritage of my father was replete with military men, possibly unknowingly influencing my father's predisposition to soldiering. His choice of joining a paratrooper unit during the infancy of that type of warfare suggests that he may have inherited a risk-taking gene, which my genetic evaluation of traits on Ancestry shows that I possess.

The presence of numerous matches for me along the above referenced family lines has posed a challenge. A son of Fanny Cooper and Thomas Monroe Taylor is probably my paternal grandfather. My grandmother, being in a military and veteran tuberculosis facility at Fort Bayard at the time of conception of my father, had sexual relations there. There is no way to know whether it was consensual. Was the man a patient, a health care worker, or an outside contractor working on building at the fort? Since the record of the year Lucille was there is no longer in existence (although other years are), it is impossible to determine patients or employees at the fort in 1922.

"There are two sons from the marriage of my great-grandparents, Thomas Monroe Taylor and Fanny Cooper. The oldest son, Jewett Horace, was born in 1894. He was a veteran of World War I, having served in the 144th Machine Gun Battalion in France during the war. After the end of hostilities, he was scheduled to board the S.S. Sierra from Pauillic, France on April 6, 1919 to return to America. However, Jewett was transferred to a Camp Hospital for an undisclosed medical reason and remained in France for two more months. Jewett boarded the Santa Eliza to return home on July 5, 1919 and arrived in Brooklyn, New York on July 20, 1919, and was met there by his father. (Records on Ancestry.com about Jewett Horace Taylor)

The younger son, David Lenwood, was born in 1902 and there is no record of military service. It is extremely likely that Jewett is my paternal grandfather, but definitive proof is not available to determine that Lucille and Jewett were at Fort Bayard at the time of my father's conception. Jewett's World War I records were destroyed in a fire, and Fort Bayard records are not available for 1922 or 1923. However, the circumstantial evidence from DNA relatives, and Jewett's military service and illness in France are strong indications for him being Arthur's biological father.

My father went to his death thinking he had found the family of his father, but dad didn't have the advantage of DNA matching to know for sure. He believed that he wasn't Fred's biological son because my Grandmother Lucille didn't deny Ronald's claim. My father lived under a cloud of deception during his childhood and part of his adult life.

What was the genetic and emotional inheritance he carried? Was the lie the source of his ever-changing identity? Did it make it more likely that war trauma would have even more of an impact due to the parental cover-up of his paternity? Research on PTSD has demonstrated that adverse childhood experiences combined with sustained combat can predispose a soldier to severe PTSD postwar.

6

DUTCH—MASTER OF REINVENTION

"Show me a man who will jump out of an airplane, and I'll show you a man who will fight." —James Gavin[1]

Dad was a restless sort. As if trying out different roles and identities, he was a combat paratrooper, a counterintelligence agent, a policeman, a private detective, a counselor at an addiction hospital, a director of alcohol and drug rehab services for various populations, including homeless veterans, teenagers, and active military. He was constantly attempting to "find himself" as if the real "Dutch" had eluded him.

In the book Emotional Intelligence, Galit Atlas posits that the undivulged experiences of our parents and grandparents can impact our mental health and sense of self. "Family secrets live inside us."[2] My father was unknowingly the repository of secrets, the eye of the hurricane where all was quiet, but swirling winds surrounded.

Dutch's childhood memories were mostly pleasant and uneventful. His parents were affectionate and involved with their four children. The oldest was Dutch, then a younger brother close in age and two sisters younger by seven and ten years. He had no reason to question his parentage. Deeply buried, though, was an upsetting occurrence, revealed during hypnosis when he was an adult. A stranger had appeared on the doorstep of his Detroit home demanding to see eight-year-old Dutch. Fred and Lucille were upset and angrily told the man to leave and never come back. Later, Dutch overheard his parents talking in their bedroom about the man being his father. It was a deeply buried memory with immediate ramifications. Dutch, not a destructive boy, was caught attempting to set the garage on fire the next day. A child's confusion was

---

1. "Honoring the History of U.S. Paratroopers," Heavendropt.org, October 29, 2020.
2. Galit Atlas, *Emotional Inheritance* (New York: Little, Brown Spark, 2022) 17.

repressed, but identity questions undoubtedly arose, though buried with a veil of silence.

When dad recounted his childhood to me, the city of Detroit loomed large in his tales. He had been born in Phoenix, Arizona, to a tubercular Lucille. Fred had married a pregnant Lucille in December 1922, only a month before the late January birth of the baby boy. Dutch spent some of his infancy on a screened-in porch under the care of a neighbor woman since Lucille was concerned about her infant son being exposed to active TB in both parents. Dutch was a toddler when his parents, now healthy, moved to Colorado near Lucille's birthplace. They remained in the West for three years and added another son, Ronald, a year after Dutch's birth. Life in Colorado was rough due to the weather and lack of employment opportunities.

In 1929, with jobs scarce due to the Great Depression, the family moved to Detroit, Michigan. Dutch spent his formative years from first grade to high school graduation as his family expanded to six with the addition of sisters Mary Ann and Elizabeth. The Motor City had been bustling in the 1920s, but the beginning of the Great Depression made for a few difficult years until the New Deal policies of FDR helped the automobile industry recover. Fred and Lucille were fortunate to be employed. Lucille worked as a registered nurse, and Fred was a welder at Budd Wheel Company, a producer of car components. The city population of one million in the 1930s supported major sports: the Detroit Tigers baseball team, the Detroit Lions football team, and the hard-hitting Detroit Red Wings in hockey. Each team had won a championship title in their sport during that decade, dubbing the Motor City also the City of Champions.

Dutch caught sports fever young; even in old age, he could recite the World Series lineup of the Detroit Tigers. When he was a preteen, he was mischievous and extroverted, the leader of a group of neighborhood boys who snuck cigarettes and committed harmless pranks, especially on the girls. He often was in trouble in his rigid Catholic school. Since nuns were permitted to use corporal punishment, spankings and being hit with a yardstick were almost a daily occurrence. He adapted by wearing two pairs of knickers to school to soften the blow.

In high school, he was a star athlete in baseball and basketball. Not content with only those sports, he took up boxing at Golden Gloves, emulating his hometown hero, Joe Louis. He won the Diamond Belt, which marked him as an amateur boxing champion, a skill that was a positive during his paratrooper war years.

The Schultz family lived in a working-class Irish/Italian neighborhood in a duplex on the east side of Detroit. Dutch was academically and athletically successful in high school. Upon graduation from Saint Philip Neri in June 1941, he was awarded a baseball scholarship to Eastern Michigan University in Ypsilanti.

There was a detour on the road to college due to the lure of joining the Civilian Conservation Corps. The Corp was created by FDR in 1933 for young men to work at improving America's public lands, forests and parks. The men lived in military-style housing, were provided with meals and paid thirty dollars a month.[3]

Dutch joined a camp in New Mexico. He had been visiting his paternal family, which consisted of Fred's mother and younger brother, Carl. Rattlesnake Springs CCC camp was about three hours from Deming, where his relatives lived. It was located near Carlsbad Caverns. The work the CCC enrollees performed consisted of tilling and landscaping the eighty acres of the camp, planting cottonwood trees, creating trails, cleaning up and maintenance of the caverns and working on the living quarters, recreation center and infirmary.[4] Dutch ran the canteen/PX and, when not working, hung out with friends at the camp. His closest buddies were Mexican Americans, and more than once, he used his boxing skills to protect them from taunting townies.

The camps were a training ground for the military, with men from diverse backgrounds living together in barracks and pursuing a single goal of beautification and conservation of American lands.

The work of the CCC was mostly stopped, with the exception of projects that aided the war effort, upon the entrance of the United States

---

3. "CCC Brief History", CCC Legacy, https://ccc.legacy.org/history-center/ccc-brief-history, accessed 11/1/23.

4. "Carlsbad Caverns National Park Historic District," New Mexico Sites, https://living-newdeal.org/us/nm, accessed 9/18/22.

into World War II on December 7, 1941. Formal statutory termination was on June 30, 1942.

The young men who enrolled to work at the camps were now standing in line to enlist in the Armed Forces. Dutch enlisted in February 1942 after a tug of war with his mother about which branch he would serve in. He wanted to be a Marine like Fred, but his mother strenuously objected. She accompanied him to the Army recruiter and strongly stated her desire that he be in something "safe." Soon he was at boot camp and anti-aircraft training at Fort Bliss and also Camp Wallace, both in Texas. No infantry training occurred. He only learned how to shoot a rifle. By October 1942, he was stationed at the Naval Yard in Portsmouth, Virginia. He did not feel like he was contributing to the war effort. His duty at the Naval Yard was to be a lifeguard at the pool where the children of officers swam. He was determined to get into a combat unit, especially since his younger brother, Ronald, had joined the Marines and was fighting in Guadalcanal. Lucille's objections to that branch did not extend to Ronald, and she allowed Fred to take him to the Marine recruitment center.

It was vexing to Dutch about the unequal treatment, so he did an end run around his mother's wishes, and as soon as he saw a recruiting poster for Airborne, he volunteered.

Only the most physically fit, highly motivated, and mentally tough made the cut in the competitive attempt to become airborne. The elite nature of the new form of warfare and the fifty dollars extra a month spurred Dutch's decision to become a paratrooper.

October 1943 was the launching point for his paratrooper training. He was assigned to the 505th Parachute Infantry Regiment of the 82nd Airborne under Lieutenant Colonel James Gavin. The training was at Fort Benning, Georgia, a locale known for its heat and humidity, hence the nickname "Frying Pan. The recruits had to live up to strenuous physical and mental expectations to prepare him for jumping into enemy territory. Exhausting hikes carrying 100 pounds, being able to engage in hand-to-hand combat, and rigorous calisthenics were required. If a man fell out, he was gone, not able to tolerate the intense demands.

Jump school consisted of jumping from a number of increasing stationary heights up to a 200-foot tower before the men were ready to jump from a plane. Dutch fainted on his first jump from the plane and had no awareness of it until he hit the ground. He completed the training and met the standard of five plane jumps at Fort Benning. Wanting to conquer his anxiety about jumping, he also jumped five more times at Camp Mackall, North Carolina. Dutch never had the love of descending from a plane connected to a parachute that other troopers experienced but was determined to prove that he was brave enough to feel the fear and do it anyway. Success in becoming an elite paratrooper was achieved by only about thirty percent of volunteers.[5]

The next stop would be Fortress Europe. Upon arrival in Northern Ireland in early 1944, Dutch joined seasoned troopers as a newbie, a replacement for the killed and wounded the 505th had lost in their two combat jumps in Sicily and Salerno, Italy. The 505th was sent to temporary camp quarters in Quorn Village, in Leicestershire, England, on February 14, 1944, a central location near the Great Central Railway, the main transportation mode in wartime Britain. Training for the liberation of Europe took place for almost four months, the men spending their nights in olive green bell tents and days practicing for battle. It was a pleasant interlude, especially for the men who had been in fierce battles in Italy in the past year. Townspeople were welcoming and warm, inviting the young paratroopers to their homes for tea, pastries and dinners.

The tough preparation for jumping into fortress Europe was to ensure the men were well prepared to be dropped behind enemy lines in the dark of night to surprise the Germans occupiers. Dutch, however, was somewhat remiss in his preparation, spending as much time on boxing workouts and practice matches as he did on combat readiness. He had been assigned to C Company of the 505th. His company commander, Captain Anthony Stefanich, approached him two weeks prior to D-Day with the unwelcome news that he might not jump on D-Day but rather be part of the beach invasion. He had done too much boxing and not enough work on combat preparedness. Crestfallen, Dutch pleaded to jump, and his Captain promised to try to make the jump happen. By the time the 505th left Quorn on May 29, 1944, on their way to Spanhoe Airfield,

---

5. Dutch Schultz, oral history.

Captain Stef had kept his promise, and Dutch had the go-ahead to jump with his regiment. The 505th arrived at Spanhoe on June 3, 1944, and set up cots in the hangers to await the go signal for the invasion of Normandy. Plans for the jump into France in the early morning hours of June 5 were scrapped due to the inclement weather. Finally, a window of clear weather enabled the invasion to commence. Early in the morning of June 6, 1944, Dutch was ready to exit the C47 along with the rest of his stick. The jump was anything but smooth. The pilots attempted to evade enemy fire and dropped 200 feet, sending the troopers to the floor. Standing up, they jumped in a hurry but were too low at 400 to 500 feet. Dutch oscillated once and then slammed into an apple tree, wrenching his back. Sore but able to cut himself out of the parachute with his prized WWI brass knuckle knife, he dropped to the ground near a hedgerow. Totally alone, he felt fear. "I was totally alone . . . I was scared as a frightened rabbit . . . I didn't see anybody, nobody, for the next five or six hours."[6] He heard a sound and aimed his M-1 rifle. Thankfully, it was at a cow instead of the enemy since he had forgotten to load the gun before he jumped.

After wandering for hours, he was finally found by Lieutenant Jack Tallerday (Executive Officer of the 505) at daybreak. Tallerday had in tow seven other lost troopers from 82nd and 101st, who were all newcomers to combat. Tallerday walked ahead to reconnoiter. An hour passed without his return. The group went down the same road and saw Tallerday on the side, pale and unconscious, with a medic attending to him. One hundred yards further, the paratroopers were exposed to mortar shelling and scattered in all directions. Dutch looked around and saw no one—he was alone once more.

Lost again and found once more by the "Jumping General" James Gavin, who always jumped with his men into combat situations. Gavin had gathered a group of troopers who were wandering alone in the hedgerows and brought them to the site of the fierce battle at La Fiere Bridge in the town of Ste Mere Eglise. The 505th needed to secure the bridge to assure that troops landing at Utah Beach would be able to move forward

6. Todd Anton, "The All American," D-Day Memory Tour, www.ddaymemorytour.com/history , accessed 2/10/23.

into interior Normandy. After two days of fierce battle, the Americans held the bridge.

The 505th was then on the move. Dutch's back injury was slowing him down. He couldn't keep up with his platoon. After two weeks of fighting through the pain, he was barely able to walk. He was sent to the battalion medical tent, and it was discovered he had severely torn liga-ments and dislocated vertebrae. Evacuated to a hospital in Cardiff, Wale, doctors advised that the injury was severe enough for him to be sent back to the States. He protested and insisted on returning to his company, not wanting to let down his fellow paratroopers. He rejoined his outfit in early July after they returned to Quorn, England, after 33 days of battle in Normandy.

Dutch's war was far from over. After he relinquished the chance to return home for medical reasons, he prepared with the rest of his division for the next battle.

His continuing war experiences have been memorialized in books by Cornelius Ryan, Stephen Ambrose, Patrick O'Donnell, Ed Ruggero, Phil Nordyke, and others. Also, my previous book, *The Hidden Legacy of World War II: A Daughter's Journey of Discovery*, detailed his combat experiences from Normandy to Germany.

However, the emotional and physical toll of this intense combat was not analyzed completely. In the Market Garden campaign in Holland, he suffered a devastating loss with the death of his beloved company com-mander, Captain Anthony Stefanich. It occurred during the first days of battle when Captain "Stef" tried to save troopers in a crashed glider, and he was killed during the attempt. Dutch's emotional repression and hardening began then—"It was the only time in combat that I broke down and wept over somebody that I cared about."[7]

Horrific and brutal war experiences were common in the succeeding months, but he did not crack. Steely resolve fueled him forward through-out the devastation and brutality of the Battle of the Bulge. Fighting through the Hurtgen Forest in early February of 1945, the 82nd came upon remnants of the unsuccessful American assault. Slowly melting snow exposed the body parts of soldiers who had been left in the bitter

---

7. Carol Schultz Vento, *The Hidden Legacy of World War II: A Daughter's Journey of Discovery* (Camp Hill, PA: Sunbury Press, 2011) p. 39, footnote 10.

cold and rough terrain. A leg, an arm, and a head were creeping out of the snow. Dutch passed out and lay motionless on the ground, partly overwhelmed by the sight and smell, partly from exhaustion and sickness. He was dragged approximately a mile to a medical tent by a lieutenant, where he was diagnosed with double pneumonia. Again, in the hospital, he left against the doctor's orders as soon as he had regained enough strength to rejoin his company. The war was coming to a close, but not before another example of inhumanity was discovered.

In early May of 1945, the 82nd came upon a concentration/work camp in Ludwigslust, Germany, named Wobbelin. Over 1000 dead bodies lay in grotesque positions, with 200 more barely alive. The stench of death permeated the air. Dutch: "I threw up . . . The images we saw were nightmares. I can't and won't describe them to you. It made those bodies I saw in the Hurtgen Forest seem like nothing."[8]

The psychic toll of repression of an emotional response to these dreadful and barbaric examples of inhumanity enabled Dutch to survive psychologically until the end of the war. But the toll on his mental health was incalculable.

Combined with his childhood of secrecy and lies about his paternity, his combat experience was an additional trauma, which made him prone to severe PTSD that followed him back to the States after the war.

---

8. Todd Anton, "The All American," D-Day Memory Tour, www.ddaymemorytour.com/history, accessed 2/10/23.

Lucille Schultz holding infant Arthur, Phoenix, Arizona, 1923.

Arthur as high school freshman in Detroit.

Mitzi and Dutch Schultz, first year of marriage, 1946.

Carol and Rosemary Schultz leaving their father at San Diego, CA aiport at the time of parents's separation, 1957.

In uniform as older man.

Dutch (wearing hat) with other Army counterintelligence agents at Frankford Arsenal, Philadelphia, Pennsylvania, mid-1950s.

Lucille Barge Schultz,
1920

Fred Schultz WWI Marine,
1919

Dutch Schultz when he was a private detective, early 1960s.

Lucille Schultz, Veterans Administration nurse, California, 1950s.

Seated: Fred Schultz's mother & stepfather, Alfons Zanon Schultz and
Marie Redding Schultz. Standing: Elizabeth and Valentine Ehrmann. Circa
1897–98.

7

DUTCH & MITZI—LA FAMILIA MEETS THE WILD WEST

"The end of World War II marked the beginning of beautiful love stories . . . as sweethearts who'd deferred marriage during the war rushed to wed in peacetime . . . 1946 is also the year of a demographic blip often overlooked: an unprecedented spate of divorces."

—CORINNE PURHILL[1]

The centerpiece atop their wedding cake features a World War II Paratrooper and his bride, a red, white, and blue ribbon wrapped around the base. Seventy-eight years later, it still stands tall, slightly faded with time. The ornament lasted decades longer than the hasty marriage in the shadow of war.

The petite auburn-haired bride, adorned in a satin wedding dress with a heart-shaped neckline, stood next to the tall, uniformed paratrooper, medals, patches, and jump boots, signifying his recent military service. December 22, 1945, was their wedding day, happening only three weeks after he returned from war-torn Europe. He came to Philadelphia, not his home, and three thousand miles distant from his parents on the West Coast. The couple had only spent a few months together after their chance meeting in 1942 until their marital preparations in 1945.

It was an unexpected romance that began when Dutch accompanied a service buddy to Philadelphia on leave and met the girl of his dreams. Expectations of perfect love and endless happiness filled their letters to each other and gave Dutch hope during the brutal battles he fought. Soon, reality collided with the fantasy of blissful togetherness. Different

---

1. "The unromantic, untold story of the real US divorce spree of 1946," *Quartz*, 6/26/18, qz.com.

cultural values, geographic preferences, and trauma of their pasts inter-
fered with their vision of perfect happiness.

The theory of emotional inheritance posits that we unknowingly
carry not only our trauma but also the emotional load of our parents
and grandparents within us, along with our unique genetic mixture. Unlike DNA analysis, which is scientifically documented, our emotional
inheritance is deep in our subconscious and has a significant influence
on our life choices.[2]

Trauma can also be inherited biologically through the process of epigenetics. In analyzing the transmission of PTSD, "Epigenetics provides a
way for environmental exposure to be 'written' on the genome, as a direct
result of gene and environment (trauma) interactions."[3]

The newlyweds had no inkling of the fierce headwinds facing them in
terms of their respective familial transmission of trauma.

The bride, Madeline, aka Mitzi, was the daughter of Italian immigrants. Immigration is an upheaval, and her parents experienced being
an unwelcome ethnic group in the early twentieth century. My maternal grandmother, Michelina, lost her father shortly after she arrived in
America in December 1911. Michele Maddalo died in August of 1913.
She then lost her husband, Luigi, when he died at the young age of
32 in Hamburg tuberculosis sanitorium in Berks County, Pennsylvania,
where many immigrants were sent when suffering from the disease. I did
not discover the truth about the disease and his seven-month stay at the
sanitarium prior to his death until the early twenty-first century when
I requested Luigi Russo's death certificate. The tale told by my grandmother and his four children was that he died from a heart condition. I
believe that the shame of tuberculosis being associated with immigrants
from less desirable countries spurred my family to lie about the true cause
of death. That was different from my non-Italian paternal grandparents,
who were forthcoming about their bouts with tuberculosis. As a child, I
was aware of their previous battle with the disease.

My mother mourned the loss of her father for the remainder of her
life. According to family lore, he doted on her, the youngest, the baby.

2. Galit Atlas, *Emotional Inheritance*, p. 17.

3. Hunter Howie, "A review of epigenetic contributions to post traumatic stress disorder,"
Dialogues Clin Neurosci, 2019 Dec; 21(4), 417-428, www.ncbi.nlm..nih.gov/pmc/articles/
PMC6952751.

Her mother told Mitzi that she would engage in imaginary conversations with her "daddy" when she was a child. Michelina married twice more, but Mitzi did not consider either of those men a father figure. The early loss led to her search for a husband who would partially fill that role. However, as she soon discovered, her new spouse had issues of his own.

Love would have a hard time conquering all for the new couple. Within the first week of their marriage, trouble brewed. They were on a cross-country train trip to Dutch's parents' home in San Francisco a few days after their wedding. During their transfer to another train in Chicago's Union Station, Dutch pulled a silver flask of whiskey from his pocket while waiting to board. Clumsily, he dropped it, and the brown liquid puddled around his feel. Mitzi was aghast and embarrassed at the stares from other passengers in the line. They finally boarded, and when darkness fell, they both went to sleep, lulled by the clackety-clack of the train as it sped across the Plains. Suddenly, Dutch, in the middle of a nightmare, bolted up and attempted to open a window, shouting, "Here they come, here they come," while aiming a phantom Tommy gun at the imaginary enemy. His wife was startled but then tried to wake and soothe her war-traumatized husband.

Once in San Francisco, they moved in with Dutch's parents and he enrolled at San Francisco State University and told Mitzi he didn't want to return East. She at first acquiesced and looked for work unsuccessfully. After two months, she was ready to leave the marriage and return home to her family in Philadelphia. She wrote in her wedding scrapbook, "It appeared that their marriage wasn't working," like so many postwar hasty marriages. 1946 was a high point for divorce in America, not surpassed until the early 1970s during the Vietnam War era.

But, on her return to Philadelphia in February, she discovered that she was pregnant. Dutch asked her to return to California. She flew back on TWA, and they lived in a one-room efficiency in San Francisco until early June, when his college semester was finished. An elderly woman needed someone to drive her car back East and hired the young couple, who then set out on a cross-country road trip; back in Philly, tensions again grew since Dutch could not find work, which was in short supply, especially for combat veterans who obviously had no transferable skill from the war to offer employers. Mitzi found a job in her field as a beautician and stayed employed until it was too uncomfortable for her in late pregnancy. To ease the financial strain, Mitzi's sister and brother moved into a small row house in the lower Northeast section of the city with the young couple.

I arrived towards the end of October 1946 in a cramped house with a minuscule no-sink bathroom, three bedrooms, and a coal-burning furnace in the bare cellar. Barely two months after my birth, Dutch left the marriage saying, "I need to find myself," symbolic of his quest for identity.

Like the swaying of the pendulum, the couple reunited a month after this breakup. They met at a restaurant in Center City Philadelphia and reaffirmed their love for each other and a wish to make the marriage work. They shared a common bond after my birth. Mitzi's wedding scrapbook now was also a baby book where she wrote, "They're both so proud of Carol, she's really holding the marriage together".

My role in saving the marriage did not last. After two more children (one of whom died a day after her birth in 1947) Dutch's career in Army Counterintelligence, which brought the family to Austria, and relatively calm years upon the return to Philadelphia, they finally broke up for good. Dutch was still drinking—I remember that he would go to the bar across the street after work and bring home two quarts of beer in a paper bag), but he was functional at home and work. Mitzi decided she wanted a divorce when Dutch informed her he was being sent to Russian language school by the CIC command since that was the emphasis during the late fifties during the heyday of the Cold War. She did not like being a military wife and had been again working as a beautician for a number of years. It was finally over. That's when the traumas of Dutch's past flared up. The shock of the divorce sent him into a severe depression and severe alcoholism. His repressed war memories and the dysfunction of the lies he had been told during his childhood combined to cause a downward spiral. He also carried the emotional inheritance of his mother, who had been abandoned, first by the death of her mother when she was twelve, and her father's remarriage when he placed her and her younger brother into an orphanage.

To further the cycle of abandonment, her first husband, Dudley Sherman, had deserted her shortly after the marriage and the biological father of Dutch had either not taken responsibility for the pregnancy or was unaware of it.

An insight into Dutch's severe PTSD, alcoholism, and near suicide after the divorce may be explained both by his sustained combat with the 82nd Airborne in WWII and the deception about his paternity that colored his childhood. "Prewar vulnerability is just as important as combat-related trauma in predicting whether veterans' symptoms of post-traumatic stress disorder will be long lasting." Of soldiers exposed to severe combat, only about 31.6% developed PTSD.[4]

Dutch did not discover that Fred Schultz was likely not his biological father until his forties at the time of Fred's death. However, that truth may have expressed itself in different ways while his parents were carrying on the deception. Dutch was the favored son of his mother, which was obvious to outsiders and Dutch himself. His brother's revelation at Fred's funeral was based on dates from military records of my grandmother showing she married Fred when she was seven months pregnant. No scientific proof from a DNA test existed. Yet, his brother wanted to shock and hurt Dutch at the funeral of the man he always knew as his father. That dysfunction in the family may have arisen from the lies, and it took the form of one brother saying to the other, "You don't really belong." Lucille's response to her son's plaintive question, "Why didn't you tell me?' was "You never asked," was an affirmation to Dutch, who then sought out the Sherman clan, who he thought was his birth family.

He did not live long enough for DNA to give a definitive answer, but through my searching for Sherman relatives, I found it. Dutch was correct that Fred was not his biological father and had the response of shock and need to explore his identity after Fred's funeral and Lucille's terse answer. The genealogist he hired gave him much more information on the Sherman line, and that seemed to help his understanding of who he was, finally finding himself. Even though Dutch was ultimately wrong about his paternity, the lie was still a childhood and adult trauma that he had been dealing with his entire life.

---

4. Association for Psychological Science, "Why some soldiers develop PTSD while others don't," *Science Daily*, 21 February 2013, www.sciencedaily.com/releases/2013/02/130221194237.htm.

The marriage between Dutch and Mitzi may have been likely to fail from the beginning. The early breakups were mended by my birth, and as time went by, the two living children they shared were not enough to keep them together. They parented well as a couple, but apart there was increased volatility in both their lives that impacted and caused major stress for their children.

8

THE BROKEN FAMILY

*"Divorce is a journey that the children involved do not ask to take.
They are forced along for the ride where the results are dictated by the
road their parents decide to travel."* —DIANE GREENE[1]

I have no conscious memory of my mother's swelling belly or my baby sister's birth when I was four. But my vivid recall is of her when she was a rambunctious toddler aboard a ship. She was the exact opposite from me—Blue eyed and blonde hair in contrast to my Mediterranean dark brown hair and eyes. Our personalities differed also. A feisty child in contrast to my shy, introverted self, this trait was on full display when we sailed on the U.S. General H.F. Callan from New York on October 18, 1952, to arrive in Leghorn, Italy, on our way to join my father in Austria. Two weeks on the Atlantic Ocean was a challenge with an 18-month-old. My mother kept Rosemary on a harness and leash above board due to fears she would climb over the railing. The large dining room wasn't a safe haven either, with my sister sweeping her little arm to push the food from her highchair onto the floor. The clattering sound drew the attention of the other diners, who looked disapprovingly at our table.

The fire drill on the ship was an adventure. The military ship's stairs were like ladders, difficult to climb. Enormous orange life vests were on each of us. My mother was struggling to get a grasp on her toddler. A sailor went to take my sister up the steps. She shrieked, screamed and kicked him, so I docilely went with him while Mom slowly and painstakingly inched her way up.

Once we landed in Leghorn, the train through the Alps was our next journey on our trip to join Daddy. He was stationed in Zell Am See,

---

1. *AZ Quotes*, azquotes.com.

Austria, as an Army Counterintelligence agent in charge of the 435th Counterintelligence Corps. This was one of the sub offices of the Salzburg field office in occupied Austria in 1952. Our living quarters were above the office where Dad and the other agents worked. The mansion-like residence on Mozart Strasse in Zell Am See most likely had been a home of a Nazi official since there were a few plates with swastikas remaining in the dining room china cabinet.

I attended first grade at the military dependents school, where I was one of 25 military kids from all parts of America. Rosemary remained home with my mother and her aide Irma, a local young townswoman who was bilingual and was an assistant to my mother aiding her in adapting to a foreign country. I loved living in the midst of the snowy Alps and played often in the gazebo in our enormous yard. Mom did not enjoy the experience as much as I did, and within the year, we returned to the small row house in Philly without Dad, who still had a year left on his overseas assignment.

Back in the States, I became very ill with Rheumatic Fever, and Dad was brought home six months early due to my sickness. Stationed at the Frankford Arsenal in Northeast Philadelphia as an agent, Dad was at home base. I gradually improved health-wise over the next five years, and Rosemary grew into a beautiful young child. Strangers would remark on her beautiful blonde hair and bright blue eyes, and she still had that exuberant, outgoing personality with which she was born.

Mom and Dad parented well together. Dad was more involved with us than most fathers were in the 1950s. After he came home from work at the Frankford Arsenal, Mom went to her job in the evening at a ten-chair beauty salon located on the second floor above a five-and-ten store. The elevated train was level with the shop. Passengers would look out onto women getting a variety of treatments, including their weekly shampoo, roller set, and hair teased and sprayed into a helmet, not to be combed through until their next standing appointment. Mom was one of the most sought-after hairdressers in the shop and worked late into the evening while Dad got us ready for bed. Both of us in the bath together gave him time to read each of us a bedtime story.

Our family seemed happy, but appearances were deceiving. Hidden from us, there was increasing tension in the marriage that resulted in

Mom requesting a divorce. Dad was given the opportunity to attend Russian language training in preparation for a possible new overseas posting. Dad relented to her demands that he not take that opportunity and left the Army and his counterintelligence career altogether.

They attempted to smooth over their differences and once again make the marriage work by moving to California to start over. The road to San Diego was supposed to be a new beginning. The Chevrolet Bel Air trunk was full of our suitcases when we left Philadelphia early on a sunny September morning to head West. Six-year-old Rosemary and I, almost eleven, entertained ourselves in the wide back seat, unencumbered by booster seats or seat belts. Interstate highways were rare in 1957; President Dwight Eisenhower had signed the Federal Aid Highway Act only a year prior. Much of our driving trip would be on state and local roads. Through the East and into the Midwest, we saw small-town America. Burma Shave signs with sayings like "Past Schoolhouses Take It Slow, Let the Little Shavers Grow" were ubiquitous. Once we reached the environs of Chicago, Route 66 was our highway further West. One of the memorable stops overnight along that historic and colorful route was the Wigwam Motel, constructed in the shape of a Native American teepee. Meramec Cavern in the Ozarks in Missouri boasted an enormous underground cave where limestone created multicolored stalactites and stalagmites that appeared to my childish mind to be huge icicles hanging from the ceiling and growing up from the floor. As a sign of the time in the fifties, the cave complex was also advertised as an "Atomic Hideout." An additional attraction at that site was the Jesse James hideout museum.

Finally, we arrived in San Diego, California, after more than a week on the road. Our paternal grandparents lived in an 800-foot pink-hued, two-bedroom, one-bath bungalow-style house; California orange poppy plants festooned their walkway and a fragrant lemon tree was in the backyard. The plan was for our family to temporarily move into Grandmom and Grandpop Schultz's house while looking for a permanent home. The small trailer under the attached wooden carport would serve as our parents' bedroom, while bunk beds were placed in the back bedroom for Rosemary and me. We were excited by our new surroundings mainly because the blue water of the Pacific Ocean was only one mile away. I was enrolled in sixth grade at Kate Sessions Elementary School, newly built in 1956 and named for the horticulturalist who was considered the "tree lady of Pacific Beach."[2] Rosemary was sent to Catholic School, the newly opened St. Brigid's. Our dad was employed as a Coronado police officer, arriving home daily in his uniform. It seemed our family was an intact unit again. But appearances were deceiving. Dad was drinking more. I remember a "bologna versus beer' episode in the supermarket between my parents, who seldom bickered or fought in front of us. A limited amount of money caused a disagreement between them over getting bologna for our sandwiches or beer for Dad.

After five months, Mom returned to Philadelphia, ostensibly to sell the Frankford house. When she returned to California, our parents informed us that they were separating, and we were flying back to Philly with Mom, leaving Dad behind. No further explanation was given.

Our reality quickly changed. The front room in the house was transformed into a beauty shop; first, the gray drywall surrounding our former living room was painted a soft cream hue. Two large, hooded dryers and the installation of a sink for the customers' hair washing were new additions. The mantle was filled with Revlon products for sale, from lipsticks to nail polish. Our green tufted sofa and chairs were moved into the dining room, the dining set disappeared, and this was our new living room. The commercially zoned shop had a neon sign in the window blinking "Mitzi's Beauty Shop." Customers who were my mother's clients at her previous employment followed her to the newly opened shop, and soon, there were women from morning to night in our house five days a week. A number came bearing pastries, candy boxes and other goodies and placed them in our kitchen to share with us and other customers.

Roomers also moved into two of our three bedrooms to aid in expenses, since dad was still in California and the child support arrangements had not been worked out. The bedroom I shared with Rosemary now included our mother. I gave up my single bed next to my sister's and moved onto a green Army surplus cot.

Our first boarders were a married couple and their baby. He had just left Army service in Japan and brought back a Japanese wife and a cute, chubby baby. Three of them were squeezed into the back bedroom

2. "Another Side of History," Pacific Beach Schools, Oct. 25, 2020, www.thewebsters.us.

and shared the tiny bathroom with only a claw-foot bathtub and toilet but no room for a sink. In the middle bedroom, an elderly woman we called Aunt Ellen moved in. White haired with a sweet, docile face and manner, she was a grandmotherly figure. The new people in our house were kind to us and would sometimes have meals with us. However, all these changes from a quieter nuclear family household required a major adjustment for us while we were still missing our dad.

These changes were mild compared to the introduction of domestic violence into our home. Disagreements between our parents were mostly hidden from the children during their marriage. But soon, a frightening scene unfolded in front of us, not from our father but the next-door neighbor man, Jerry (aka Lee Walls). Rosemary and I called him Devil Man because of his flaming red hair and empty pale blue eyes when he looked at us. He brought intimidation by gun into our world. Our mother had been dating him after the divorce. He lived with his frail, ailing mother, Nancy, on the bottom floor of the corner row house that had been converted into two apartments. He disliked us and showed it with a scowl and pursed lips when he spoke to us. But he looked at our mother with lust and was obsessed with her. After six months, she ended the relationship, partly due to his treatment of her children and his possessiveness.

The breakup ignited a fury within him. He walked into our unlocked door while my mother was doing a customer's hair. As he entered and walked into the shop, he told the customer to leave, and he pulled a gun from inside his jacket. We were on the stairway to the upstairs bedrooms and stood there open-mouthed as he put the gun to our mother's head and shouted, "If I can't have you, nobody can!" Mom's response was, "Take me on the porch so the children don't see you shoot me." The customer, Claire, scurried us upstairs and called the police. By the time they arrived, Jerry had left after my mother pleaded with him not to kill her. There was no follow-up or investigation into him or his threats.

Decades prior to the passage of the Violence Against Women Act in 1994, there was scant redress for women who were stalked, sexually abused or victims of domestic violence. Jerry's aggressive behavior continued with harassing phone calls, following our mother on the street and pulling a gun on her again, and threats against her children. She

took action on her own, retaining a lawyer to send a warning letter to
him. On September 30, 1959, Center City Philadelphia attorney Frank
Marolla, Jr. wrote:

> I am informed by Mrs. Madeline Schultz, whom I represent,
> that you have been annoying her by the numerous phone calls
> that you have been making to her home at all hours of the day
> and night, accosting her on the street and making insulting and
> derogatory remarks and generally conducting yourself in such
> a manner as to cause her, and her children, anguish and distur-
> bance. In addition, your various veiled threats upon her and her
> children have been noted. I call upon you to immediately desist
> from this conduct and demand you do nothing in the future, to
> molest her or disturb her, otherwise, immediate action will be
> taken against you. I trust that this will not prove necessary, as
> any action that may be taken will be costly to you in time and
> money.

This was the beginning of a high state of anxiety for Rosemary and
me. Our father had not returned from California yet. Would we also lose
our mother?

9

THE CONSTANCY OF CHANGE

"Nothing is permanent but change." —ELBERT HUBBARD[1]

Along came Joe.

The next man who appeared in our lives was a gregarious Italian American in his mid-thirties. He was a gym owner, bodybuilder, and masseuse to the stars at the upscale Claridge Hotel on the Boardwalk in Atlantic City during its heyday in the early 1960s. Luxurious hotels, a bustling Boardwalk, and Steel Pier, in the era before casinos, with attractions like the "Diving Horse," dances, and big-name singers, drew large crowds to the seashore resort. Stars like Frank Sinatra, who was a regular at the 500 Club, Marilyn Monroe, and Ricky Nelson stayed at the "architectural masterpiece" of the historic Claridge.[2]

Our mother had rented a small apartment in Atlantic City for the summer, and we would take a bus there on weekends, leaving the heat and haze of the city behind for a few days. Mom's friends, red-haired Joan and backward-talking Danny, owners of a small grocery store, shared the cramped apartment with us. They would appear late Friday evening, laden with fresh fruits and vegetables, lunchmeats, pasta and snacks, enough food to feed all of us for the weekend.

Mom's boyfriend Joe would show up after he completed his masseuse duties, sometimes bringing a souvenir, a silver pitcher Frank Sinatra had touched, or a glass from which my teen heartthrob Ricky Nelson had drunk.

Lazy summer days had Joe joining us on the beach, helping build our sandcastles and teaching us how to swim under the breaking waves. We would remain on the beach until 6 or 7 PM with dinner from a

---

1. Felix Shay (1912), *The Fra: A Journal of Affirmation*.
2. www.claridge.com.

blue cooler full of food and drink situated under the beach umbrella. Once in a while, Rosemary and I would get an ice cream treat from the white-clothed "Fudgie Wudgie" man. That name reflected the refrain he called out as he trudged through the hot sand, carrying a heavy icebox - "Getcha Fudgie Wudgie here."

I was thirteen, and mixed with my fun was embarrassment at the swimming attire of my mother and Joe. Her leopard print bathing suit with the straps untied to avoid tan lines and his black Speedo were too revealing for me as I was dealing with my newly developing young teen body. I flinched and wanted to hide when Joe would hike Mom on his shoulder for a photo shoot.

Back home in the city during the week, my newfound interest in politics was sparked by my fascination with the handsome, dynamic Presidential candidate John Fitzgerald Kennedy. I was eagerly awaiting the Democratic National Convention in which Kennedy was a leading candidate for the nomination. Joe and I had a bet; I would win if Kennedy were chosen as the Democratic standard bearer. My reward would be a late-night South Philly cheesesteak from "Pat's-King of Steaks." Obviously, I won the bet, and he kept his promise; all of us, including my just awakened 9-year-old sister, drove through the quiet streets of Philadelphia at midnight to get my prize.

Joe and my mother married in November 1961 in Arlington, Virginia. Trouble came a few months after the wedding in the person of a man dressed in a dark brown monk's robe, a burlap belt around his waist from which hung a large shiny black rosary. His name was Father Sylvester Catallo, a Capuchin Franciscan friar/priest. The Capuchins not only took the vow of celibacy but also simplicity and poverty in order to serve the needy. I was in an adjoining room and heard the priest tell my mother to end the marriage because she, as a divorced woman, was the cause of his brother living in sin and putting his soul in mortal danger. Joe, son of Italian immigrants, had not yet told his mother of the marriage, and Father Sylvester dramatically said it would "kill" her if she found out. Within a year, Joe and my mother were divorced due mainly to his family's objection. And just like that, Joe was gone.

Our dad returned from California soon after mom's second marriage imploded. Rosemary and I would go with him on weekends to movies, swimming, and miniature golf; Dad was living with his paratrooper veteran buddy Joe Tallett and his family in a house in Bucks County and working as a private investigator in a firm he, Joe, and another former paratrooper had formed. The next couple of years were relatively peaceful. Mom and Dad were both unattached and cordial with each other.

The peaceful interlude ended in September 1964. We were impatiently waiting for Dad to pick us up on a crisp autumn Sunday morning. Then, instead of our father at the door, Joe Tallett appeared with the shocking news to us that Dad had gotten married to a woman that he met recently in St. Luke's alcohol rehab center. Unbeknownst to us, he had been at the center for two weeks, drying out from a bender. There were subtle signs over the past couple of years that he was drinking more. He came to my sixteenth birthday party tipsy; he never showed up (later, I found out he was drunk and very depressed) to see me in my sparkly white dress before I left for senior prom. But these were isolated incidents, and not being in the same house, we didn't realize how deep he was into alcoholism. He was no longer functioning well. The detective agency was falling apart since his partners could no longer rely upon Dad.

His new wife was Ardelle, a former model, who was an alcoholic also. When Dad came back to Philadelphia in October, he moved into her center city Philadelphia apartment which is where we first met her. She was a tall, leggy brunette with expressive, large brown eyes and a model's figure. She tried to put us at ease by showing us newspaper clippings from her modeling days. Most of them were poses in her underwear, only slightly revealing since Victoria's Secret and risqué bras and panties were not yet on the scene. However, Rosemary and I squirmed nervously as we viewed the clippings. Seeing Dad's new wife in her underwear, even though it was sedate, was unnerving to two Catholic schoolgirls who had been instructed not to wear black patent leather shoes. The rationale for that prohibition was that the shiny shoes would reflect our panties like a mirror.

A few months passed with minimal contact with the newlyweds. Evidently, they had both fallen off the wagon and were drinking again. Sobriety was elusive, and this marriage of two active alcoholics almost ended in disaster in January 1965.

It was a dreary and frigid January evening. Mom was on a date, and I was awake to answer the ringing of the phone close to midnight. Dad's sobbing and trembling voice scared me as he kept repeating, "I missed the boat. I've been a failure as a father." He then said Ardelle had slit her wrists in a suicide attempt and was bleeding in the bathtub. Drunkenly, he said he was going to join her and kill himself. With a quavering voice, I begged him not to do it and told him he was a good father as I tried to talk him down from following through on his suicidal desire. He seemed slightly calmer when he hung up the phone. I sat on the front steps, shaken and pale to waylay my mother. She arrived soon after the call and immediately called Joe Tallett, who was my father's savior, many times over. When Joe arrived at the apartment, Ardelle had been taken by ambulance to the hospital. Possibly, my dad called the police, or a neighbor in an adjoining apartment heard the arguing and screaming. Joe contacted my grandparents in California and put Dad on a plane to San Diego to live with Fred and Lucille.

Ardelle had been sent to Norristown State Mental Hospital outside Philadelphia after her unsuccessful suicide attempt. Lucille sent for Ardelle upon her release to join my father, who was living in my grandparents' old white trailer under the carport. Ironically, it was the same trailer my parents shared during our stay in San Diego seven years prior. The reunited couple was on a committed search for sobriety and attended Alcoholics Anonymous meetings almost daily.

Rosemary and I had minimal contact with Dad, consisting of occasional letters and presents on birthdays. From his correspondence, we learned that he was attending college at California Western University through the GI Bill, and Ardelle was selling makeup in a department store.

I was a commuter student in my junior year, working my way through college, and Rosemary was a junior in high school the next time Dad reappeared.

I heard his voice before I saw him. Engaged in conversation with an older man on Broad Street at Temple, he walked past me without recognition. I was too shocked and upset to stop him, aware that he did not contact his children, especially knowing that I was a student at Temple, to make them aware of his return. Once again, Joe Tallett was the conduit between my mother and father, telling Dad that he walked past me on campus.

Ardelle and Dad had returned to begin employment at Eagleville Hospital, an inpatient facility for alcoholics and addicts. Dr. Donald Ottenberg, the medical director, had transformed the former tuberculosis sanitarium into a badly needed treatment center for the underserved population of alcoholics and drug addicts in the 1960s. My father and Ardelle moved into an apartment in Conshohocken and would meet us occasionally for dinner.

The next few years were relatively peaceful, with no major upheavals. Dad was offered the position of Director of a residential alcohol and drug addiction treatment program for young people in the bucolic Bucks County suburb of Philadelphia. He and Ardelle moved into the main house, and residents lived in bungalows on the property.

On the days my sister had off from high school, I would have her accompany me to Temple. She was now 4 inches taller than me and turned heads with her bright blue eyes, strawberry-blonde hair, and well-proportioned figure. She resembled the All-American prototype of the sixties, the "Breck Girl" with her long, luxurious mane.

A male acquaintance of mine at Temple was immediately attracted to her. Four years older and more worldly, he pursued her and despite the concerns of my mother and myself, they began dating steadily. Robbie was the first controlling boyfriend in her short life. He was possessive and jealous, but she clung to him, relishing his attention, perhaps as a replacement for her "sometimes" father. Dad had been gone from the home and her daily life for more years than he had been in it. I had experienced the best years of our parents' marriage, 11 years with dad in the home.

Rosemary's choices in men were reflective of her emotional trauma with the upsets in her young life and the heritage she carried from the losses our parents and grandparents had experienced. An episode with Robbie and Rosemary eerily reminded me of a similar situation with my mother and Jerry, aka "Devil Man." The gun was replaced with a hammer and fist. My mother went to a "Single Parents' dance while Robbie was sitting on the front porch tightly clasping a red-handled hammer in his hand, waiting for Rosemary to return home from a night out with a few friends. I was left to control the situation and defuse Robbie's anger. She exited a blue car, which hurriedly sped away when they saw the hammer. Rosemary ran to the door, and Robbie angrily followed. Fuming and red-faced, he went into the beauty shop area with her, screaming, "Where were you?" When she didn't answer, he punched a large hole in the shop drywall. Next, he grabbed her by the arm and dragged her to the front door. I took hold of her other arm and, pulling her back, shouted, "She's not going anywhere with you"! After a minute of tug of war, he relented and left, muttering curse words to himself.

Robbie called the next day, apologizing profusely, and they remained a couple into her freshman college years. She chose Temple even though she had a state scholarship for tuition to any Pennsylvania college and an Economic Opportunity grant that would have paid for room and board. Temple was her choice because Robbie was still there.

Their relationship ended during her freshman year, and she seemed lost after that. She first moved out of our mother's house and into the *Today* program with our father. The inability to co-parent successfully was on full display then, with my mother constantly bemoaning that Rosemary had left her. I was so tired of hearing my mother's complaints, which I felt were unreasonable since my sister was with her other parent. When Rosemary came with our dad to collect some clothes, we began arguing, an infrequent occurrence since we were each other's biggest supporters.

Rosemary eventually left Today "in the dead of the night" and without notice according to our father. She moved into a series of apartments on her own, before she ended up with the man who would be partially responsible for the untimely end of her short life.

10

FOREVER YOUNG (BOB DYLAN)

"The loss of a brother or sister is not small, unimportant, or invisible . . . It's quite the opposite . . . 'the loss of a lifetime' because who else do we have relationships with that stretch our entire lives?"

—Lynn Shattuck[1]

Was Rosemary especially emotionally vulnerable due to the chaos in her life? Was she predisposed by epigenetics, environment, and emotional inheritance of trauma from parents and grandparents?

The answer is elusive. Twenty-two years, barely an adult, her life was over. No time for introspection, to look back on a life well or poorly lived.

Her last chapter began at a Philly club, Artemis, a glittering hip spot decorated with an assortment of antiques. It was there she met Tom (alias). She was on the rebound from the end of a relationship with a medical student for whom she had deeply cared. Tom pursued her avidly, sensing her fragility. He was a self-titled artist with few sales, a wannabe psychic and a master manipulator. Rosemary was hooked quickly and, within a few weeks, moved into his apartment in a renovated brownstone on the perimeter of Center City Philadelphia. Tom had dirty blonde longish hair, an indolent manner, and an arrogant attitude, evidenced by the snapping of his fingers if he wanted to get your attention.

Rosemary was just beginning her junior year of college in September of 1973, carrying a full load of credits and working 15-20 hours a week at a newly opened Old City bar and restaurant, Khyber Pass, decorated with Afghan wedding tents and samples of Pakistani clothing, and serving drinks on an antique 1876 bar. Rosemary, a waitress and all-around

---

1. *Things I Wish I Had Known When I Became a Grieving Sibling.*

helper, became friends with the owner, a colorful woman from the Main Line named Serrill Headley, who opened the establishment after she fled Pakistan, where she had moved after marrying a Pakistani diplomat. Finding the strictures on females too binding, she left not only her husband but also her two children behind.

While Rosemary was juggling a full course and working many hours, Tom was attending one class at Temple and working minimal hours at an art supply store, scheming how to make money off Rosemary's face and figure.

A talented professional photographer and fine arts painter, Frank Bender was Tom's acquaintance. Upon Tom's request, he took partially clothed photographs of Rosemary posing seductively to send to Playboy magazine located in Chicago, Illinois, in the early seventies. The hope was that she would be selected as a Playmate for a barely dressed centerfold for the girlie magazine. In a sense, she would be Tom's cash cow. (Frank Bender, in later years, would become a widely known forensic sculptor for his skill in identifying the "forgotten dead and apprehend the fugitive living."[2])

Not surprisingly, my sister's beauty and body were well-suited for *Playboy*. An all-expenses paid trip to Chicago for a centerfold photo shoot was in her future. My reaction was disbelief that she would accept the offer. It was 1973, and the feminist movement was in full bloom. The idea she would bare her body for men around the country to lust after was upsetting to me. I was one of the few female graduate students in a Political Science Ph.D. program at that time and was determined to make it in a male-dominated world, so I disagreed with her choice. She resisted, increasingly influenced by Tom, and became adamant with me that she would be a Playmate.

I wasn't able to convince her. My Italian American Catholic mother had no awareness of the plan that would have caused fireworks to extend through the entire extended family. Finally, my sister wrote to my father, who had now returned to California to live. He gingerly dealt with the issue by advising her to make her own decision but be aware of the consequences of men viewing her as a sex object and the unwanted attention she would attract. That worked, and she eventually declined the offer.

---

2. *New York Times*, July 30, 2011.

Thanksgiving Day, November 22, 1973, was unseasonably warm in Philadelphia. My Italian extended family all gathered in the Northeast neighborhood of Mayfair to join in a traditional feast. The area was relatively new compared to other sections of the city, with much development occurring right after World War II. There were green manicured lawns in the front, an attached garage and a larger size row house. The home of my mother's older sister was the site of many family gatherings. Rosemary and I went on a walk, taking advantage of the nice weather. She had arrived with Tom, a passenger on the back of his Yamaha motorcycle. Our conversation revolved around the tenth anniversary of JFK's assassination and the television specials memorializing his death. Her offhand remark that "JFK was too perfect to live" still haunts me in light of what occurred that night.

She hugged and said goodbye to all the family. Little did we know that was the last time we would see her alive.

At 3 AM on November 23, I was awakened by the insistent ringring-ring of the bell. As I rushed to the door, I could see the figure of a policeman through the glass. His question as I opened the door was, "Does Rosemary Schultz live here?" We were living in the upstairs apartment of a duplex with our mother habiting the first-floor residence. I answered yes (she had not changed her driver's license address). He walked in and requested to make a phone call. My mother and I thought she possibly was at a hospital when, on the phone, he asked, "Where is she now?" Our hopes were dashed when he turned to my mother and coldly stated, "Your daughter is dead."

I immediately fell to the floor screaming. My mother ordered, "Carol, stop it." I did and went into rescue/caretaker mode to comfort my mother. Suppression of my grief enabled me to soldier on and perform the necessary tasks. I called my aunt and uncle in the middle of the night, and they came rushing to our house. My next job was to call my father, who had recently moved back to California. He began sobbing loudly, repeating no over and over again. He called me back after making plane reservations to Philadelphia and said he would arrive in a couple of days.

The next morning, our doctor came to the house and gave my mother a sedative injection. While she slept, I was on to my next duties: call people to tell them about the death, pick out a casket, and select family funeral flowers were on my list. I had just turned 27 and was operating on autopilot, never having dealt with the death of anyone young before.

My aunt and uncle accompanied me to a coffin warehouse in North Philadelphia. There were so many choices, 30 styles in a large, cavernous room, ranging from metal in gold, bronze, silver and black and wooden caskets from dark cherry to light-hued pine. My eyes rested upon a sole white metal casket in a corner. I chose that because, in an alternate reality, I would be with Rosemary, aiding her in finding the perfect white wedding dress.

Stein's florist in Northeast Philadelphia was the next stop. The "Dear Beloved Daughter" casket spray was a mixture of roses, carnations, and lilies. I burst into tears when I had to choose a sister floral remembrance, my stoic demeanor façade disappearing for a moment.

The final stop was to the Morgue/Medical Examiner's facility. My father had arrived in Philadelphia, and we entered the grim-looking building, which was unnervingly near Presbyterian Hospital, where she had arrived DOA. The accident occurred at 11:30 PM on Thanksgiving night on West River Drive in Philadelphia next to the ornate and historic Strawberry Mansion Bridge that spanned the Schuylkill River. The motorcycle, which had been weaving in and out of the lanes, collided with a car whose driver had been drinking. The two drivers responsible for the crash both survived, but Rosemary flew off the back of the cycle and violently hit a road sign, causing a fractured skull and multiple injuries to the torso and legs.

We were handed the last remnants of Rosemary's life at the morgue— a watch with a blood-stained band, her purse, blood speckled with a torn strap, and dangly earrings, one of which was twisted into an odd shape.

Duties completed, it was time for the viewing and funeral. I was numb standing with my parents, looking at my dead sister and thinking, *We were supposed to grow old together*. My fear that my mother and father would fight at this time was unfounded, thankfully, but I dreaded the road ahead without my ally. Many showed up to pay their respects, but the details are a bit blurry to me now. I do remember Joe, my mother's second husband, appearing and my telling him that he was good to us. His reply as he gazed at Rosemary with tears in his eyes was, "Not good enough." My father had his latest girlfriend accompany him from California. Even though he was still legally married to Ardelle, the woman who would become his third wife was ever-present during those tragic days.

The day of the funeral would have been appropriate for a movie scene. A light misty rain, trees barren of leaves, and a throng dressed in black surrounding the while coffin ready to be lowered into the ground, Rosemary forever silenced. My journey through the "loss of a lifetime" had begun.

The nightmares began about a month after her death. She was in danger, ready to drown or fall off a cliff; in my dream, as I tried to save her, she slipped from my reach. My guilt and sense of responsibility survived her passing. Since she could toddle, I was told to be responsible and take care of her. The parentification took hold, and I played the surrogate parent role well until I failed. My mind knew I could not have stopped the events that led to her accident, but my heart and conscience would not absolve me. Therapy has helped me learn to manage the loss, but all these years later, I still question, "What if?"

11

CONCLUSION

"The past is never dead. It isn't even past." —WILLIAM FAULKNER[1]

The feeling I had was insistent. It was an energy spurring me to understand what had happened in the lives of my grandparents and parents and how it impacted me. Carl Jung noted that there is an impersonal trauma within a family that is passed . . . to children . . . I had to complete things which previous generations had left unfinished."[2] The secrets, losses, and heartaches of ancestors are not erased but rather remain in the genes and memories of a later generation.

Two generations of stories were passed down to me, but important truths were not revealed. When I sent in a DNA sample to Ancestry and 23 & Me, I hoped to determine whether my uncle's callous remark about my father's paternity at Fred Schultz's long-ago funeral was correct. Was Fred my biological grandfather, or was it the wayward Dudley Sherman? To my surprise, it was neither man. Two surnames, Schultz and Sherman, which weren't mine by kinship. I had to discover and include that hidden piece of my identity to fully understand all parts of the family dynamics that were passed down to my late sister and myself.

Thus began a deep dive into researching the family history in detail to understand the losses and traumas, but also appreciate the resilience. Shame and guilt were likely underlying the secrets and deceptions, but unintended consequences arose from lies.

Lucille hid the identity of her son Arthur's biological father. Whether his conception was a result of a consensual relationship or a sexual assault at Fort Bayard will never be known. The losses and abandonment

---

1. —*Requiem for a Nun*, New York: Random House, 1951.
2. Carl Jung, *Memories, Dreams, Reflections* (New York: Crown Publishing House, Random House, 1963).

Lucille had experienced, with her mother's death and her placement in an orphanage in her early teens upon her father's remarriage, must have caused her to crave security and protection. She did not find that with her first husband, Dudley, who deserted her, but Fred came to her rescue.

Fred's upbringing by his stepfather, Al Zanon, may have made him sympathetic to Lucille's plight. It is unknown whether Fred was aware that Al was not his biological father until later in Fred's life since he was listed as native-born in Deming, New Mexico, numerous times on official documents prior to 1940.

Lucille had two marriages and a child with another man. It began a generational cycle of three, which was passed down to her eldest son. My father was also married three times to Madeline, Ardelle, and Gail.

Coincidentally, a generational cycle of three also existed in my maternal line. My grandmother, Michelina, was widowed by Luigi; a few years later married Angelo D'Anselmo, and after their separation and his death, married Nick Marino. My mother, her youngest child, also had three marriages: to Dutch, to Joe, and Lee Bondy.

In these marriages of my grandparents and parents, it was their final marriages that lasted the longest. It may have been their ages at the time of those marriages, or possibly their emotional needs were finally met. My father's last marriage was to a flight attendant who satisfied his wanderlust and enabled him to travel. My mother married someone who was extremely attentive and loving towards her, almost in a paternal fashion.

In an alternate reality, I would be having a conversation with my sister about how this family story impacted us. Sadly, that conversation is impossible, but by writing, I can share the story in hopes that my understanding of intergenerational trauma and emotional inheritance will resonate with others.

The secrecy about my father's paternity was the most egregious. It was a lie by omission that caused family dysfunction that led my uncle to blindside my father at Fred's funeral with that information, even if my uncle had no way to prove the validity of it, just from his viewing of his mother's VA records. It was a hurtful statement, probably engendered by Lucille's obvious favoritism towards her eldest. Adverse childhood experiences, such as secret paternity, combined with war trauma, have been shown to make it significantly more likely for severe and long-lasting

PTSD in combat veterans. Dutch fit into this category, which led to alcoholism, divorce, and periodic abandonment of his children post-divorce from Madeline.

As previously noted, the abandonment issue was present in my grandmother Lucille's life. Sent away to a Catholic orphanage at 12 or 13, she, in later years, sent her daughters away to a Catholic boarding school for their high school years. His mother's repetition of her experience being sent away may have colored my father's limited contact with his children after his second marriage. This was evidenced by his return to Philadelphia from California after three years and not informing his children that he had returned to the city where they lived. He was at the college he was aware I attended and walked right past me on Broad Street at Temple University without recognizing me.

A major loss occurred in our family prior to my sister Rosemary's birth but after mine. The loss of an infant at two days old in 1947 must have been a tragedy for our parents. I was a year old and had no conscious memory of it, but I knew about the death of baby Mary Ann at a young age. The genes of my parents may have passed down that memory of that tragedy. During my mother's pregnancy with Rosemary, there must have been significant worry and anxiety about the upcoming baby.

Our nuclear family was dysfunctional. Children take on different roles to adjust to the dynamics of that type of family structure. I was the caretaker, the parentified child, the eldest daughter responsible for my younger sister and taking on adult responsibilities after my parents' divorce. I felt protective of my sister, and the sense of guilt and grief was sometimes overwhelming because I felt I failed in my responsibility, even though, rationally, there was nothing I could have done to change the dynamics that led to the accident and her death.

Rosemary was the lost child, emotionally sensitive, and also the rebel in her later years, not afraid to follow her desires. Her susceptibility to controlling men may have been due to her father's absence in her formative years. Depression was part of her later years, although she hid it well. After her death, I was surprised at her diary entries mentioning death: "I'd like to die. Not that I would ever kill myself, but I'm curious to know what happens . . . I'll study now so I'll become 'educated,' and one day, my brain will rot in the ground along with billions of other people."[3] Children who have adverse childhood experiences are prone to depression and possibly early death due to risky behaviors.[4]

Rosemary never had an opportunity to find a way to recognize her strengths or to feel resilient. However, my grandparents and parents, in their long lives, were able to demonstrate resilience in their lives. My grandmother, Lucille, was able to have a long and successful nursing career and a stable marriage of 43 years. My father stopped drinking in 1964 and was a recovering alcoholic for 41 years, working in the drug and alcohol addiction field as the director of various programs throughout his career. Fittingly, his last position was at Fort Irwin, California, where, as the director of addiction services, he helped many soldiers who were struggling with similar issues he had experienced.

As for me, I was lucky. My position in the family, both nuclear and extended maternal Italian, was a protective factor in creating resilience. I received the best years of fathering when my parents were married, and my father was present in the home and quite involved for a father in the fifties. In my early childhood years, extended family either lived with us or close by and family members doted on me. In addition, I was a prolific reader, often using books as an escape from reality. However, I was not unscathed. My body kept the score, a process noted by Bessel van der Kolk. At a relatively early age, I experienced severe hypertension, which has required four different categories of medications for many decades. It has been noted that "a trauma is stored in somatic memory and expressed changes in the biological stress response," which can cause "continued physiological hyperarousal."[5]

We are not untouched by trauma, but it doesn't have to control our lives. We can adapt, move forward and understand the traumatic experiences by looking through the lens of previous generations. Understanding helps develop compassion and empathy for our grandparents and parents, as well as for ourselves.

---

3. Rosemary Schultz, Diary, May 6, 1970.
4. "Reversing the 3 Lifelong Consequences of Adverse Childhood Experiences," *Presence*, Oct. 18, 2021, https://presence.com/insights.
5. B.A. van der Kolk, "The Body Keeps the Score: Memory and the Evolving Psychobiology of posttraumatic stress," *Harv.Rev.Psychiatry*, Jan-Feb 1994, https://pubmed.ncbi.nlm.nih.gov/9384857.

ABOUT THE AUTHOR

CAROL SCHULTZ VENTO is a former Political Science professor and an attorney. She received her undergraduate degree in Sociology, Master's degree in Public Administration, and doctorate in Political Science from Temple University. Her law degree is from Rutgers University School of Law. She is the daughter of World War II veteran Arthur 'Dutch' Schultz, the 82nd Airborne paratrooper portrayed in the 1962 D-Day movie *The Longest Day* by Richard Beymer. Dutch's war experiences have also been written about in a number of books about the European Theater in World War II, including those by Stephen Ambrose and Patrick O'Donnell. Carol is the author of *The Hidden Legacy of World War II: A Daughter's Journey of Discovery*. She has also written numerous annotations for *American Law Reports*, 5th and articles for Defense Media Network (www.defensemedianetwork.com).

Carol is a native of Philadelphia and currently lives in Palmyra, New Jersey with her husband Frank.

Find Carol Schultz Vento at:

Facebook: (1) Carol Schultz Vento, Author; (2) DaughtersofD-Day
Instagram: csvento
Twitter/X: @ddaydaughter